The Waiting War

FINDING YOUR "YES" IN HIS "NOT YET"

JENNA OAKES

ISBN 978-1-0980-7000-7 (paperback)
ISBN 978-1-0980-7002-1 (digital)

Christian Faith Publishing, Inc.
832 Park Avenue
Meadville, PA 16335
www.christianfaithpublishing.com

Printed in the United States of America

Let this be written for the generation to come,
so that those yet to be created may praise the Lord.
—Psalm 102:18 (ESV)

CONTENTS

FROM ONE WARRIOR
TO ANOTHER

"Your summers are always so blessed, aren't they?"

Aly was sitting in my favorite recliner as we enjoyed cheesecake, coffee, and quality time while her son napped in the other room. I had just let her read a chapter of this book and given her more details on how God continued to pour out when I sat to write. As she reminded me how wonderfully intimate my summers with Jesus always are—months where time stands still in my elementary teaching schedule—my soul settled into the couch with a thankful heart. The summer of 2019 was quite an exciting and humbling journey, as the Lord called me to record all He taught me over the previous year.

It was the last day of May. I was blow-drying my hair, trying to decide what I wanted to order at dinner that night. Suddenly an idea completely unrelated to food flooded my mind. It's as if I clearly heard the words "Finding your yes in His not yet," followed by eight topics related to this theme. The moment was so blissfully heavy and overwhelming that I had to stop what I was doing and write it all down. I have never experienced such a quickening of the spirit, such an undeniable call in my entire life. It was incredible—a moment in time that I will never forget.

After my adrenaline settled, all I could think was, "A book? That's a whole lot of words! I don't have a whole lot of words." True, one of my lifetime goals has always been to write a book and have it published. I've written personally for most of my life, and I even started an inconsistent blog a few years back to practice writing skills. True, the Lord has used words repeatedly to draw me closer to His heart. Others have even fueled this dream with their encouragement, but the reality still remained—I had no idea what I could write about to fill so many pages. Who was I to write a book for the glory of Jesus?

The truth is, I am nobody special. There is nothing extravagant or unique about my life. I am not the kind of person you would look at and say, "Of course she's writing a book!" But y'all, Jesus, He changes everything. He qualifies the unqualified. I have been adopted by the King. Alone, I am nothing; with Him, I am royalty. I am a warrior. I am chosen, highly favored, and a force to be reckoned with because of the simple fact that I am His. I have prayed for years and years that God would take the painful, joyful, embarrassing, and shameful moments of my past, present, and future and use them for His glory. I pray He will use this book to do just that.

I'm always very hesitant to say things like "God told me" or "God said" because I never want to misrepresent Him by putting words in His mouth. But I want to make sure I communicate just how intimate and raw my writing sessions with Him were. I sat down each afternoon with a hot cup of coffee and absolutely no plan as to what details each chapter would hold. Day after day, my heart and story poured from my fingertips, seasoned with tears of joy and awestruck thankfulness for what He has done and continues to do in my life. I still look at this book and am dumbfounded that He would choose to share this message through me of all people.

I don't pretend to have an arsenal of knowledge about the Bible. I have no seminary degree and no formal ministry experience. I don't have the gift of prophecy. I have never had a near-death experience where I met Jesus face-to-face and returned to tell about it. What I do have is my own copy of the Bible that has become my lifeline. I have a hunger to intimately know my Savior, who took residence in my heart on the third Friday of August in 2009. I have heart-wrenching tales of the battles I have waged against my flesh, tales that I so badly wish all ended in victory. I have a desire to bring glory to the name of Jesus through my story, one that continues to unfold day by day.

When I study the Word, I am well aware that I read it through twenty-first-century eyes. I acknowledge that knowing the societal norms and culture of that day hold incredible value when digging into scripture. Understanding the syntax of ancient languages and the complexity of historical contexts sheds a whole new light on the scripture we read. These chapters, however, are written as I often relate to and learn from scripture—by putting myself in the shoes of the characters in these stories and comparing their responses to my own. This method never fails to deepen my understanding. It always fuels my personal growth, because girl, the Bible (even the Old Testament) is still very much alive and applicable today. It is insane how the struggles we face here and now trace back to the very beginning of time. As you read these chapters, I pray you join me in seeing through the lens of self-imposed empathy.

The point in all of this—this book and, ultimately, our sanctification journey—is to unearth the parts of our soul that need to be acknowledged and healed to become more conscious of our flesh-driven tendencies and to become more raw and real in our relationships with the Lord. So I challenge you—allow the prompts and questions at the end of each section to drive you out of comfort zone and into freedom. Dig deep, sister, far beyond surface-level responses. Enter your secret place with the Lord and take the plunge into the vastness of your soul, even if it's painful to do so. Grasp His sovereign hand and dive headfirst into all aspects of your life. Trust that Jesus cares deeply for who you are, down to the very last beautifully broken detail. Consider it all—from your environment and beliefs to your emotional perspectives and various relationships, from the realities of your past to the expectations of your future. And when you're tempted to shy away from a particular area, burying it deep inside your soul again, I encourage you to bow up against this well-laid plan of the enemy. Wrestle with it until it's buried at the foot of the cross instead.

If you happen to be digging into this content collectively, I want to encourage the introverts to be brave and bold and the extroverts to be mindful of the privacy others may need. Whether you read this on your own in your pj's or with dear friends in a nearby coffee shop, I challenge you to be open and honest with yourself and your fellow prayer warriors.

Then as you finish reading each section, I urge you to pray. Using Priscilla Shirer's PRAY acrostic (Praise, Repent, Ask, Yes)[1] found in her book *Fervent*, I have included a handful of prompts for you. Once you fill it out, I encourage you to talk intimately with God about it all, using the response prompts as a guide. This is another area in which I want you to dig deep. Be mindful that Satan doesn't want you to take the time to do any of this. If he can busy your mind and heart enough to keep you from entering into your secret place with your Savior, he will be successful in keeping you trapped in your personal hamster wheel of emotions. Don't let that happen.

Finally, each section wraps up with a list of scriptures related to what has been discussed. Know that these barely scratch the surface of what God's Word has for us regarding the topics, so if these verses don't speak life into your mind and heart, I encourage you to seek out the biblical promises and truths that do. Either way, I want you to commit to memorizing one verse related to each topic. By the end of the book, you will have eight verses committed to memory. When the gnawing lies of the enemy try to rise up and choke you, these verses will be your weapons. Combat the lies by speaking the scriptures out loud or reading them when the battle rages wildly inside you. Read and recall them often, so they will stay

---

[1] Priscilla Shirer, *Fervent: A Woman's Battle Plan to Serious, Specific and Strategic Prayer* (Nashville: B&H Publishing Group, 2015), Page 21–23.

fresh in your mind. Personally, I prefer to put verses on a note-card and tape them to my mirror. When I have memorized one, I move it to a wall in my closet. Every morning, as I brush my teeth, I read my wall of verses again to keep them fresh in my memory. If nothing else, put those suckers in your phone and pull them out when life feels like it's weighing you down. Figure out what your trick is and commit to it, even when Satan is sneaky and tries to distract you. I don't know about you, but I am so tired of falling prey to his manipulative attempts to rob me of my joy and confidence in the Lord. We just don't have time for his nonsense anymore, y'all.

As you begin turning these pages, know that I am praying over our time together. I pray that the words you are about to read will affect you, simply because they are God-inspired. I pray that only the biblically sound seeds of my story will take root in your heart, so the name you're left clinging to is *Jesus*, not *Jenna*. I pray against the schemes of deception that Satan may have planned. He is the master of manipulation and will attempt to twist these words as you read them. Ultimately, I pray against anything he may say or do in this life to hinder your progress toward abundant life and freedom in Jesus.

Friend, whoever you are, wherever you are, know that I also *praise* the Lord for you, not simply because you found your way to this book, though I am thankful you did. I praise Him for the incredible plans He has for your life and for giving you a curiosity to know His heart more intimately. I praise Him because He is using each step of your surrender to create a ripple effect of undaunted, heavenly hope in this fallen world.

I pray this book ignites a fresh Holy Spirit fire inside you, leaving insatiable hunger for more of Him. I pray that the Holy Spirit anoints each word that you read so that this message falls on your heart in a unique, individualistic way. I pray that the Lord would use this book to fill you with unapologetic freedom, restorative peace, irrepressible joy, and audacious confidence.

I pray for you—plain and simple.

I may not know your name, but He does, and that is more than enough.

I pray that as you wade through your own journey of waiting, this book will help you discover your freedom song of "Yes!" in the midst of His mysterious "Not yet."

Battle I:
When Plans Change

READY, SET...WAIT

"And that's my ten-year plan," I finished with certainty. My professor gazed at me and smiled, not an excited, impressed smile but one full of compassion and wisdom. She took a deep breath and said, "That's quite a plan. Just remember, sometimes plans change, and that's okay. Sometimes it's even a blessing." I smiled and humbly acknowledged her response, as unenthused and skeptical as it sounded.

It's funny how those who have walked the road before us usually know best (and by "funny," I mean completely irritating, though reassuring). As it turns out, my plan did change. As I write this, I am in year nine of the decade-long plan, and the only part that has seen its way through is my marriage.

You may ask what happened to the other parts of the plan. No, I didn't settle, become lazy, or hightail it in the opposite direction out of fear. The reality is that my dreams haven't disappeared. I still dream the same dreams—of being a published author and hearing the ocean from my kitchen window, of working full-time for a Jesus-loving nonprofit and being able to give extravagantly without a second thought, of inhaling the salt-kissed breeze of the Irish Sea and dancing in the streets of Spain. These dreams are all still very much alive in my heart, but God has also birthed new dreams in me. I dream of being an exceptional wife and having a marriage that would make Old Hollywood envious. I dream of seeing a great awakening take place in my generation and seeing every person in my life experience salvation and a fresh fire from the Holy Spirit. I dream of being transformed into a true Kingdom woman—a woman of excellence and all it entails.

I dream of being a mother.

Before you're tempted to roll your eyes and convince me that I've let passing time kill my "real" dreams, remember that I didn't say I have given up on or replaced those ambitious dreams of my doe-eyed, the-world-is-my-oyster, nineteen-year-old self. I merely said that God has added to and reprior-itized the list—not society, not my husband, Brock, but God—just Him. How did this shifting of priorities and discovery of new dreams begin?

The short answer is *change*. My life has echoed the theme of constant change, most frequently in my adulthood. Growing up, I craved the stability and independence that being grown would offer. I often dreamed of the day when I would finally have a family of my own and a home that would be our retreat in the midst of life's chaos. How ironic that my prince charm-ing would be everything I ever dreamed of in a godly husband yet bring with him such a definitive promise of change.

We spent the first few years of our marriage moving around with his career, which kept us from planting our roots in any one spot. This was not part of *my* plan, and I often reminded the Lord of that! Looking back, I marvel at how God used those years to establish a solid foundation for our marriage and a kingdom perspective in our souls. With each heart-wrenching uproot and transfer, the Lord taught us to lean a little harder on Him and each other. With every bittersweet "See you later" to new friends, He taught us how to love people well instead of loving fleeting aspects of our lives, such as places, houses, and hobbies. Through all of the pruning, my heavenly Father patiently taught me how to embrace His leading, grow with it, and thrive in it. He taught me to chase after His heart before my own. He taught me to surrender my timelines and practice unwavering trust and confidence in His will.

At least, I thought He had.

When we began our journey to grow our family, I jumped in with both feet—with zero hesitation. Our perspective had always been that we would love to have children of our own, but we didn't need kids to fulfill us or give our life and marriage purpose. We were ready for whatever God had planned for us, even if that wasn't kids. We both acknowledged that we never saw having children as the only way to leave a heavenly legacy in this life. Plus, we knew how drastically our lives would be altered once we had tiny humans running around.

We waited five years before deciding that we were comfortable with the idea of little feet pitter-pattering through the house. Though we were well aware that He could have called us to parenthood at any time, we chose to take measures to wait, because we wanted to use what little control (we thought) we had to plan responsibly. In our eyes, the gift of children was one of the sweetest, most valuable blessings to be given. We wanted to honor that gift by making sure we were as confident as we could be—spiritually, emotionally, physically, and financially—when we stepped into our roles as parents.

Adding to that, we are also all-or-nothing people. When we do anything in life, we give it our best or we don't do it at all. We're both wired that way, and it is glorious! God knew we each needed another go-getter for a spouse to pump us up and propel us forward. All that to say, when we did decide to start actively trying for children, we were convinced we were ready. I was excited. I was hopeful. I was all in. I just knew that God would honor the fact that we tried to do everything we could with what we had been given as we turned the page to begin this new chapter of our lives.

Our first negative pregnancy test was on Christmas Day. Though I was a little bummed, I was not surprised or disheartened in the slightest. I had done the research and knew that it could take months to conceive. I was focused on the positives—we were healthy, we were finally in this new phase of life, and God was going to pour blessing upon blessing into our little family.

Seven negative tests later, I sat confused and frustrated. Did we not do our part? Did we not honor You in every way possible? Did we miss something? Don't You want us to have children? You know they'll be raised as kingdom kids. You gave us these desires after all! Are You even listening?

I thought back to the hopeful, expectation-free perspective I had when we began this journey and tried to determine when my heart started to take its eyes off the true Author and write its own story. I had repeatedly said that I trusted Him, His will, and His timing, but here I sat, my heart crying out in defeat. I know, I know, there are people who have tried far longer than seven months. Trust me, other people reminded me of that quite often.

While we're on the topic, I'll let you in on a secret: knowing others have endured childlessness for longer DOES NOT magically transform these thoughts and emotions! I will never understand how the thought of other women facing years of heartache is supposed to be encouraging. To all of you who are a friend to someone struggling through this specific area of waiting, for the love of all the queso in the world, take my advice and be a safe place for them. Comparing your friend's unique journey to thousands of others (even with the good intention to motivate and bring a fresh perspective) makes it seem like you see their feelings as unjustified and—dare I say it?—ridiculous. When you choose to take this approach, you end up doing nothing more than diminishing the other person's desire to be open and honest with you. In the end, not one ounce of that healthy point of view healed their heartache, sweet cheeks. (Steps off the soapbox.)

When I took my frustrations to Brock, his eyes focused on mine—full of the same compassion I had seen in my professor years earlier. The woman he would move mountains for was standing before him with a discouraged heart, and he had to lead her back to the cross with tenderness and grace. He didn't try to change my perspective by comparing our journey to others. He didn't try to help me come up with solutions and next steps to try. He didn't encourage me to mope and wallow in my emotions. He didn't even try to use his own knowledge and point of reference to give me a new outlook on the journey. Brock knew the only thing we had to cling to for guidance during this battle of emotions was the Word of God, so he rose up as the leader of our household and dropped a biblical-truth bomb into our conversation.

"Sweetheart, I know you don't want to consider this right now, but what if it isn't God's plan for us? I'm not saying it won't be, but what if it's not? What if God has brought us together to accomplish something for His kingdom that requires us to NOT have children? We have to remember that we aren't here to live checklist lives. We're here to fulfill a purpose that is far bigger than ourselves. If God gives us children, it will be wonderful! But if He doesn't, there will be a reason, and life will still be beautiful, and He will still be good."

First, praise God for this gift of a kingdom man in my life—one who is bold and fears only the Lord, one who keeps his eyes on Jesus and pursues the greater calling of joy over shallow happiness, one who loves me enough to lead (and sometimes drag) me back to the cross.

Secondly, Satan is a butthead. I fell for his manipulation and distractions. I was so caught up in the fact that our chapter (read "my plan") was not on track that I took my eyes off the Author of our entire story—the One who was there from the beginning, the One guiding us in the middle, and the One already standing at the end. When I lost focus, reckless emotion took hold of my heart, and I started sinking deep into the murky waters of doubt, anger, and fear. I started perceiving my situation through entitled eyes.

I allowed the idol of control back into my life—the keyword being *allowed*. I allowed it to dictate where my purpose would be rooted and where my joy would flow from. I allowed it to draw my focus away from submitting to the Father's will. I allowed myself to be distracted by me. I made the choice, whether intentionally or not, to let my thoughts and desires run free instead of taking them captive and making them obedient to Christ (2 Cor. 10:5, NLT). Those emotionally charged thoughts became habitual, eventually throwing me into a downward spiral. The humble and grounded outlook I started this ride with had slowly and deceitfully morphed into a shackle around my heart.

Sure, if you had asked me at the time, I would have told you that I was completely okay with whatever God was up to in the waiting. Even when I confessed the conflicting emotions stirring within my heart, I always claimed that I was going to lay them at the cross and give it all back to Jesus. I didn't even see Satan's stealthy plot to distract and derail my heart, mind, and body. (Yes, they are all intertwined.)

During these months of roller-coaster emotions, unmet expectations, and changed plans, God would teach me what true surrender actually meant. I don't say that as the typical buzzword *surrender*. Trust me, I thought I knew what it meant, but I was wrong.

Perhaps "active surrender" is a better way to phrase what we are called to practice—what I was *not* doing. Active surrender is more than just orally relinquishing control over thoughts and emotions that we battle. It's unimaginably difficult and humbling. It strips away any previously effective facade and brings you face-to-face with the cluttered junk that's built up in the closet of your heart.

In the heat of this refining fire, God promised to reveal parts of my heart and mind that desperately needed to be healed and made new—parts I didn't realize were decaying, ones that I didn't even know existed. It was sobering to realize how desperately I needed the Lord to work on my heart. It was even more sobering to realize that I didn't have the unwavering faith and trust I originally thought I had.

I was terrified of the level of surrender Jesus was calling me to. I wasn't afraid He would ask me to drastically step out in faith and refocus my eyes on Him—that would have been simple, comparatively. No, I trembled because I knew He was preparing to expose silent parts of my soul that had been hidden (quite well, might I add) for so long. The Lord was planning to show me what truly dying to myself meant. He was going to bring me to a place where my weakness was laid bare, where I was finally done chasing after the things I thought I wanted, where my spirit screamed, "I want you more!"

Brock's questions echoed in my soul. If not, will life still be beautiful? Will my heart still cry "Yes, Lord"? Will He still be good?

What were my honest answers to these questions? I knew what I was supposed to say, how I was supposed to feel, what I was supposed to think. But even if my mind knew the truth, did my heart believe it? I knew my heart would always be deceitful (Jer. 17:9), but wasn't it, at the very least, obedient?

I had to be honest with myself, and truthfully, I was embarrassed by what I found—I was the epitome of a hypocrite. I was seemingly open, honest, and raw with those around me, all while lying to myself about who reigned supreme in my heart. My lips praised Him, but my heart was far from Him (Matt. 15:8).

I had a choice to make.

I could choose to run from the fire looming ahead, ignore the pressing to call my own bluff, and refuse to follow my husband back to the cross. I could keep attempting to connect the dots and hope I didn't spiral further into anger, anxiety, obsession, and depression.

Or I could abandon my idea of what I thought life would look like at this point in our journey. I could trust that whatever was waiting on the other side of the flames would be far sweeter than anything I could have dreamed up on my own. I could discover what it truly means to abandon myself and confidently cry, "Yes, Lord."

MARY, JESUS'S MOTHER

"I'll land at ten thirty on Thursday."

Brock lived and worked in West Virginia during our last year of dating. He was flying home for my college graduation, and we were trying to coordinate the festivities with his arrival. Since he was arriving so late in the day, we didn't have to plan too much, other than making sure we were available to pick him up from the airport.

Little did I know that he had been working with my mom and best friend to plan his proposal. I assumed he meant ten thirty at night because he worked such crazy hours. They somehow managed to keep it under lock and key, and he pulled off an incredible surprise entrance and asked me to be his bride. Pure bliss!

I lived on cloud nine during the six months between his proposal and our wedding. Everyone was so excited, and I was simply giddy. The actual planning part didn't tickle my fancy, but the anticipation of standing next to him on our big day was constantly at the forefront of my mind. I'd often find myself daydreaming of our wedding, our tropical honeymoon, and settling into our first home together. I would think about what life would be like as newlyweds and being able to say, "My name is Jenna *Oakes*, and this is my *husband*, Brock." I would think about our future adventures and what we would name our someday children.

Until recently, I had never considered that Mary might have also spent hours daydreaming of her anticipated life with her soon-to-be husband, Joseph. Of all the times I've read the story leading up to Jesus's birth, I've never once stopped to consider the events through Mary's eyes. Putting myself in her place, even while reading through twenty-first-century lenses, gave me such mad respect for her. What the Bible shares with us doesn't expound upon the details in regard to Mary and her fiancé, so I'm going to let my mind wander a bit. Remember, I haven't spent hours researching this story in Scripture. I'm reading my Bible, imagining what it was like, and going from there. Take a minute and just imagine this with me. Will you?

The Bible doesn't give us an exact age, but we know Mary was in her early teens when she was engaged to Joseph. Assuming there was love between them and no one was being forced to the altar, it may be safe to say that Mary felt some level of excitement. Maybe she dreamt of the way Joseph would look at her when they were married. Would he cry joyful tears when the time came? What would their bridal week be like? Would they always live in the town in which they were married? How many children would they have? Boys? Girls? What would they name them? What would their personalities be like? What would their family be like as a whole?

That's all pretty relatable. We can see ourselves doing that, right? Now imagine you're lost in a daydream and an angel shows up right in front of you and says, "Greetings, favored woman! The Lord is with you" (Luke 1:28). Y'all, I'd fall right off my chair, maybe even pass out! I like to picture Mary making bread during this moment and knocking the bowl over into a cloud of dust as she falls backward. Are you visualizing this? We know that Mary was startled because the story continues by saying she was confused and disturbed. I imagine she was trying to make sense of what in the world the angel meant (Luke 1:29).

He keeps speaking to her, saying, "Do not be afraid, Mary, for you have found favor with God" (Luke 1:30). *Who? Me?* I don't know about you, but if an angel of the Lord showed up in my kitchen and told me I had found favor with God, I'd be awestruck. I'd probably be grinning ear to ear and have tears of joy streaming down my face. I'd probably feel overwhelming peace and excitement overtake my body. I'd really like to believe I wouldn't attempt to take a selfie with him. But seriously, can you even picture that? Now that you've settled into this moment, let's keep going.

The angel continues, "You will conceive and give birth to a son, and you will name him Jesus" (Luke 1:31). If I were Mary, nearing my wedding day and thinking of my future, I would have been thinking, "Having children couldn't be too far off for us. It's still an overwhelming idea, but this news is nothing out of the ordinary for a bride-to-be." So why the angelic announcement? But obviously, I'm not Mary. And I don't know exactly what she thought that day. However, I do know she gathered that this would all come to fruition before her wedding took place, because she immediately responded by asking, "How can this happen? I am a virgin" (Luke 1:34). I wish so badly that the Bible further described Mary's response.

Did she pace the room?

Did she tremble?

Did she sit dumbfounded? Curl up in the fetal position and hum?

I have to wonder if she panicked.

I'm sure the whole angel-in-your-living-room, you're-being-told-you-will-give-birth-to-and-raise-the-Savior thing would be completely staggering. At some point, she undoubtedly realized that this could potentially cause a hiccup in her relationship with Joseph. I don't know how I would respond to this realization. I can't imagine how I would tell Brock this news. I can't imagine how I would tell my family. Would he believe me? Would they? I can't imagine the storm that would result, the whispers and judgment to ensue. More than all of that combined, I can't imagine my middle-school-aged self having to process it all. Whew.

Let's loop back once more to Mary's initial encounter with the angel. After he tells her that she would give birth to Jesus, he continues to speak about her future son.

"He will be very great and will be called the Son of the Most High. The Lord God will give him the throne of his ancestor David. And he will reign over Israel forever; his Kingdom will never end" (Luke 1:32–33). I wonder if Satan tried to whisper in her ear that she wasn't cut out for this calling. I wonder if he tried to throw her age and lack of parenting experience in her face. Maybe he reminded her that she would potentially lose her fiancé and family forever.

There are times in my life where my heart screams, "WHO AM I TO DO THIS?" (like being called to write this book, for example). I know this is a common struggle for a lot of people—most women I talk to, actually. Can you imagine the magnitude of pressure Mary might have felt once she digested this news?

Then there's the whole "How can this happen? I'm a virgin" thing. The angel told her, "The Holy Spirit will come upon you, and the power of the Most High will overshadow you. So the baby to be born will be holy, and he will be called the Son of God" (Luke 1:35). I can't begin to fathom what was running through her head at this moment. First of all, she's a virgin. She had to already be a little nervous about her upcoming marriage and the kind of vulnerability it would entail. But now?

Now I'm not suggesting, even for a millisecond, that she was physically intimate with God. I don't know how the biological logistics went down, but that's precisely my point. Do you know how much confusion and nervousness she had to feel at the thought of surrendering every last part of herself for the glory of her God?

At this point in our story, the angel has now finished speaking. Mary has yet to respond in any way other than to ask how. Before we keep going, I want you to take a minute to really pause and consider this moment—standing face-to-face with an angel, digesting this life-altering news. How would not just you but middle-school, about-to-be-married you have responded?

I'd like to think that I would have responded with boldness and confidence, that I would have completely trust the Lord's plan. More realistically, however, I would have probably panicked and started asking question after question. I would have probably worried myself into sleeplessness. Truthfully, I'd probably have had moments of self-pity because it *wasn't* supposed to happen this way.

Scripture tells us very simply how Mary reacted. "[She] responded, 'I am the Lord's servant. May everything you have said about me come true'" (Luke 1:38). Does that make your heart sink like it does mine? Here is this middle-school girl who lived at a time where pregnancy out of wedlock was a huge no-no (to put it lightly), who was set to soon be married and begin her life and family, whose plan was about to be wrecked, and she responds boldly, trusting God without a second thought. She is willing to potentially lose everything in order to fulfill the role God is calling her to. That, my friends, makes me respect and admire her on a whole new level.

I could go on for days about what I've learned from Mary's life. This chapter didn't even begin to dive into her giving birth to or raising the Messiah. It didn't even mention her watching from afar as He stepped into His ministry and was then tortured and crucified for the sake of the very ones who brutalized Him. Then there's her experience of watching her Son's resurrection and ascension to the Father. Jesus, her baby boy.

What an amazing woman of God, y'all. Reading her story and trying to process how she must have felt gave me a deep respect for her. Comparing her response to my hypothetical one made me check my own heart and its submissiveness to the Father's will for my life. It made me rethink my knee-jerk reaction to question, analyze, and worry about the changes to our story. It motivated me to be more intentional in my response to God's leading. Then I discussed it with Brock.

When I told him I was planning on writing about Mary and how her plans were so drastically changed, he whipped around and said, "Mary? I would think Joseph would make a better point for that." Over the next few minutes, he dove into the story from a man's perspective, and I have to say, it was enlightening. Don't get me wrong, I had considered it before, but hearing it flow from my husband's heart with the same passion I felt from the woman's point of view gave it a whole new meaning. Still, I don't try to pretend I understand what our men go through. They deal with their own unique set of pressures. But here is my attempt at relaying Brock's heart on this matter.

In Matthew 1, the story starts the same. "[Jesus'] mother, Mary, was engaged to be married to Joseph. But before the marriage took place, while she was still a virgin, she became pregnant through the power of the Holy Spirit" (Matt. 1:18). Brock asked me if I realized how Joseph must have felt hearing this news. This is where it can be helpful to insert yourself into the story; it helps you relate to the people within these narratives. If you're a woman reading this, I want you to take a minute to imagine hearing this news as a protective sister or friend. Imagine your brother or friend comes to you and tells you about this. What would you think and feel? How would you respond?

"You know Mary, my fiancé? She just told me that she's pregnant. No, it's not my child. Whose? When I asked her, she told me that she was still a virgin. That an angel came and told her that the power of the Holy Spirit would make her conceive. She says she's supposed to name him Jesus and that He is going to be the Messiah."

Girl, be honest! You know good and well you would tell him to avoid that chick as if she were sushi from the gas station down the street! It's like Brock said—there's no way Joseph wasn't completely skeptical after hearing this. After all, he wasn't with Mary when the angel appeared and told her. His heart had to be broken too. I'm sure he felt betrayed. Not only did it ruin Mary's reputation, but it also caused Joseph to lose respect in the eyes of others. Poor Joe.

27

Verse 19 continues, "Joseph, her fiancé, was a good man and did not want to disgrace her publicly, so he decided to break the engagement quietly." This is where I feel like we can see the depth of his love for her. I have no doubt he felt angry about the whole situation, yet he chose to end their engagement quietly to avoid humiliating her further. Brock raised his eyebrows and shook his head at this. He said, "Jenna, I honestly can't say if I'd respond that respectfully. He was a good man."

As he was preparing to break off the engagement, scripture tells us that the Lord appeared to Joseph in a dream to reassure him. "Joseph, son of David, do not be afraid to take Mary as your wife. For the child within her was conceived by the Holy Spirit. And she will have a son, and you are to name him Jesus, for he will save his people from their sins" (Matt. 1:20–21).

Now imagine waking up and replaying that in your head. I know part of me would feel relief that Mary wasn't lying. The other part of me would wonder if that was real or just that I ate too many snacks before bed. I know I would probably analyze the whole experience for days; maybe I would even talk it over with my closest friends. I'd probably toy with the thought of ignoring it completely and pretending it didn't happen. I mean, we're talking about a guy marrying a girl who is carrying someone else's child—a child who was going to be the Messiah. If Joseph went through with this, he would be responsible for parenting the Savior of the world. He would have to deal with the whispers and ridicule from others that came right along with this crazy commitment. That just sounds like a whole lot to deal with, and he wasn't legally bound to it yet. I'm just sayin'.

Joseph was a wise man, though. He knew not to run from God. The Word says, "When Joseph woke up, he did as the angel of the Lord commanded and took Mary as his wife" (Matt. 1:24). Their obedience amazes me, y'all. Joseph obviously struggled with the situation from a human perspective, but as soon as the

Lord spoke to Him, he didn't waste another second hesitating or doubting. When he *woke up* from his dream, he took her as his wife. No debating. No talking it over and praying about it for a few months or years. No considering how this would alter his plan. The Lord called, and Joseph obeyed—no questions asked, just as his bride-to-be had done. When I think of their radical faith despite the unknown, it empowers me to throw fear to the wind and boldly declare "Yes, Lord" when He calls.

CONNECT

What sentence, paragraph, or fact from this section stuck with you most? Reference it below.

Why did it stand out to you? What primary emotion did you feel when you read it?

REFLECT

What change are you facing in your current season of life? How has this change positively or negatively impacted what you thought life would look like?

What has been your response to this change and its impact on your life? How has your response affected those around you? Has it influenced your situation as a whole?

RESPOND

PRAISE. Name four specific praises in this season of your life.

1.

2.

3.

4.

REPENT. Regarding your current season of change, name three ways your thoughts or actions have been flesh-driven instead of Spirit-driven.

1.

2.

3.

ASK. Name two things that you need The Lord to help you fully accept, even if you feel like you're not ready or don't want to surrender them yet.

1.

2.

YES, LORD. Name one action or step you can take today to practice active surrender in this season.

1.

CLING TO SCRIPTURE

Be strong and courageous. Do not be afraid or terrified because of them, for the LORD your God goes with you; he will never leave you nor forsake you. (Deuteronomy 31:6)

Jesus Christ is the same yesterday, today, and forever. (Hebrews 13:8)

"For I know the plans I have for you," declares the LORD, "plans to prosper you and not to harm you, plans to give you hope and a future." (Jeremiah 29:11)

And I will give you a new heart, and a new spirit I will put within you. And I will remove the heart of stone from your flesh and give you a heart of flesh. (Ezekiel 36:26)

Which verse did you choose to commit to memory and utilize during your active surrender? Record it below.

Battle II:
Manipulating God

EXPECTANT SURRENDER

"NOW can I play with the dinosaurs?" One of my rambunctious, persistent students looked at me with the most hopeful eyes as he pleaded his case. He had asked multiple times during the day, and each time he was met with some form of "Not yet."

"We have other things to conquer before we can play."

"It's not time to play with dinosaurs. You know what our daily routine looks like."

"Sweetness, you know good and well that when it is time, I will tell you. Have I ever let you miss out on the fun before?" He wasn't having it.

"But...but...I did my morning work. I did my math centers. I've been nice to my friends. I've listened to you the first time you've asked. I didn't run in the halls. I've done EVERYTHING. Why can't I play with the dinosaurs? Just for a minute?"

At this point, he was leaking crocodile tears on my desk. As much as it hurt my heart to see him sad, I knew what was best for him in that moment. Even though he was politely persistent in asking, it wasn't time yet. He had to trust me. The reward was coming soon enough, but for now, he had to wait. He would have to continue to focus on the completion of his assignments and our tasks for the day, whether his heart understood the reasoning or not.

Can't we all be like this student at times? I'm always humbled when God uses these sweet souls to remind me how I am prone to treat Him. With my students, I often find myself frustrated with their doubt, fear, chaos, and challenges. It never fails—when these emotions arise in my heart, I feel the

Holy Spirit nudge me and quietly whisper, "It's not fun, is it, beloved? Show them grace. You know how they feel."

It's no secret. I have been known to try to snatch the reins from God. I am as scheduled, color-coded, and organized as they come, which can easily fuel the idol of control in my life. When it has dominated in the past, my desire to control has led to severe anxiety, which bled into every area of my existence. Knowing this, I now have to be intentional with frequent self-reflection to make sure my controlling nature is quieted. Because, girl, it doesn't matter how many different colored pens and tabs you have, you can't plan for every hiccup in life. (You listening, Jenna?)

Luckily, God knows and loves the quirks of my type A personality and has often sent lightning-bolt confirmations when I've been at a crossroads. When I first started walking with Him, this would happen frequently. He knew my tendency to overanalyze, and He would graciously calm my heart again and again with these clear signals. From decisions about relationships, jobs, and homes to future conversations, expenses, and opportunities, He has never left me questioning what steps He intends for me to take. Every time I've quieted my mind, thrown my hands up, and let Him take over, He has opened my eyes and heart to embrace His prompting. Even when His leading wasn't what I expected, He has helped me to follow through and obey. We've had a lot of lightning-bolt stories in our marriage as well. Humor me for a few pages as I share one of them.

During the first few years of our life together, we moved pretty frequently due to the nature of Brock's job (remember that promise of change I referred to in the last section?). We were newlyweds and had been living in a small town right outside of Birmingham for a little over a year when we found out we were being transferred to Jasper.

We had never heard of the town that sits forty minutes northwest of Birmingham. When we searched for information about Jasper on the Internet, Tallulah Bankhead, crime, and an old zombie show was all the information we could find. (I have to throw this in, though—that's not all there is to this small town. We absolutely fell in love with it and the people who live there to the point that we truly mourned when we moved away.) The heart of the town is less than ten miles wide, which makes it quaint yet leaves it with limited renting options. We prayed, with us needing to relocate quickly, that God would open only one door, revealing where He intended us to live during our time there.

Brock and I called a few realtors only to find that there were no rental homes available. Not easily discouraged, I rallied my troops (i.e., my mother and aunt) and ventured to the first apartment complex. Unfortunately, there was a waiting list that was pages long. The best they could do was add us to the list and call us if something opened up.

When we left, I was a little bummed but not completely discouraged. After all, we had prayed for only one open door so this must not have been it. At the next apartment complex, we found availability, budget-friendly prices, and a quick move-in date. We also found unfinished and run-down apartments, bugs, and neighbors that made us uneasy. Have you ever had an experience where you just knew in the pit of your soul that something wasn't right for you? Where you felt so uneasy that you couldn't even entertain the thought of following through? These were our gut responses to this location. We took the application, smiled, and scurried away. It may have been available, but it was obviously not the place for us.

As we ventured to the third and final option, we had an extra pep in our step. Surely this would be the answer we were looking for. It wasn't. There was nothing available for us to rent. Realizing the only option was the one that made us sick to our stomachs, we headed to meet Brock for lunch and fill out the application. We physically couldn't fill it out, though. I couldn't even eat. All I could think was, surely, *surely*, this isn't where we're being called to live.

Physically, mentally, and emotionally exhausted, we headed back to the second complex to turn in our forms. My mom and aunt decided it would be a good idea to fill out the forms at the first complex as well just in case it would bump us up on the waiting list. When we arrived, the two of them went in to fill out paperwork, but I sat in the car with a migraine, feeling completely defeated and frustrated. All I kept praying through tears was, "Why? Just why? But if this is where you really want us, we'll go. I'm trusting you to take care of us."

My mom came out and told me that the property manager wanted to show us one of their units. Y'all, if looks could kill! I was so incredibly done with that day. The last thing I wanted to do was fake a smile and tour a nicer unit that we couldn't live in. After some motherly persuasion, I got out of the car and toured with them out of politeness, but my heart was still pitching a fit. As the tour wrapped up, the property manager asked, "Do you like it?"

"It's beautiful," is all I could reply, heart aching and stomach knotting.

"If you are still interested, it's all yours," she said.

My brain was spiraling. *What? Did that really just come out of her mouth?*

"What about the waiting list?" I asked.

She replied, "I've been meaning to call you all day. Things have been so busy around here after coming back from the holiday break. You're right, there is still a waiting list, but as soon as you left this morning, I couldn't stop thinking about you. God has kept you on my mind all day. I think He wants me to give you this apartment."

I literally fell to my knees and wept, not for dramatic effect but out of sheer relief. I praised not just for the apartment but for God's faithful provision and this woman's sensitivity and obedience to the Holy Spirit's leading. I could write for days of stories like this. God has always shown up in one way or another when I stop trying to figure everything out and trust that He will provide exactly what I need.

As we entered this new season of trying to grow our family, I was so excited and full of hope. If I'm completely honest, I had been downplaying my desire for years. Everyone, including Brock, had no idea. Was this some form of twisted protection over my heart? Was I trying to curb my yearning to be a mother out of fear that it wasn't in His plan for us? I'm not really sure. All I know is that, for years, I had been quietly suppressing the butterflies that rose at the mere thought of tiny toes and baby bellies.

It's funny. I never thought I would crave this gift like I do, but when we started trying it was like the floodgates of my heart were flung wide open. The desire overflowed into every inch of my soul. The longing had become so vast, the daydreams so vivid. Disguised as confidence and excitement, I didn't recognize the idol of control when it took up residence in my heart.

When the fifth test came back negative, I started to feel defeated and angry. We were doing everything I could think of, from logging cycle data in my fertility app to well, you know. As I sat stewing and trying to figure out the missing piece, it was like God had thrown cold water in my face and revealed the unwanted house guest in my heart. I had snatched those reins from Him yet again. How in the world could I ask God to bless this journey when I was holding it captive and refusing to give it up?

I sat back and reflected on all my human attempts to control this outcome. What did I need to give back to Him to be truly surrendered? I sat down with my wise counsel—my sister-friend and my husband—and confessed. I shared how deep my desire truly was. I named my fears. I admitted to trying to control the situation. I recognized that these were all symptoms of resisting the Lord and His (read "not my own") timing. Having named the shackle and each link of the chain, I boldly declared that I was going to surrender this to Him, "for real this time." I was going to stop obsessing about the when and how of our journey to have kids of our own, and I was going to trust that His plan was perfect for me, for us.

In the following weeks, I made a conscious effort to take ahold of my thought life. Whenever fear, obsession over data, or jealousy threatened to consume me, I counterattacked the enemy's schemes with scripture. I made a choice not to allow those thoughts and emotions to take root. Instead, I practiced thinking of things that were joyful and brought life to my mind and heart (Phil. 4:8). I finally felt a peace in my spirit that had been missing for so long.

Then the sixth negative came. I was angry. I was hurt. I was heartbroken. I wailed, "What gives? Did I not do what you've called me to do? Did I not confess? Did I not give it to you? Have I not been taking every negative aspect of my mind captive? WHAT DO YOU WANT FROM ME?"

"Your true surrender," the still, small voice whispered.

At first, I rolled my eyes, banged on my imaginary microphone, and thought, "Is this thing on? Am I talking to myself over here? What do you think I've been doing?" After I had cooled off, I realized what He meant.

Yes, I had been practicing obedience. I had confessed my heart and inward grappling. I had resolved to give it back to God and had followed through with my actions. However, my motive had been manipulative and selfish. I can see that now. He knew that too. After all, "All of the ways of man are clean in his own sight, but the Lord weighs his motives" (Prov. 16:2, NASB). If we're brutally honest, somewhere in the back of my mind I thought, "Okay. Now that I've surrendered this, He will reward my obedience with a positive pregnancy test."

Before you scoff, I ask you to really look inward to those abandoned, cobwebbed corners of your heart that you let no one, even yourself, see. How many times have we declared

"I'm going to give it to God and let Him handle it" but speaking from a heart of manipulation instead of faith? How many times have we proclaimed surrender before when it's coupled with an expectation that God will hold up His end of OUR bargain? How many times have we said "I'm taking the high road, and God will handle it" with a raging heart instead of submission and trust?

This brings us back to Brock's pivotal question, "What if He doesn't?"

What if you surrender this to Him, and you never see the outcome you prayed for?

What if He doesn't save your loved one from themselves?

What if the money doesn't come?

What if the stress continues to threaten your peace?

What if they still walk away?

What if the dream you've dreamt doesn't come to fruition?

Did He still handle it? Is He still good? Is He still God?

It's a hard pill to swallow—realizing just how wicked our hearts can be, how sneaky and manipulative human nature is, and how we can be so silently hypocritical that we even fool ourselves.

When I found myself face to face with the ugliness of my soul, it was humiliating.

And terrifying.

And heartbreaking.

And peaceful.

I knelt before my God, filth wholly exposed, and said with the most humble heart I could offer, "I'm giving this dream back to you. Whatever you have for me is what I want. Whatever you have for me, even if it's not this dream, will be okay." *O God...please make it okay.*

In reality, my heart was sobbing. It's painful to let go of a dream, especially after you've finally allowed yourself to dwell in the sheer joy of it. It's painful when you realize you may never receive this gift and letting it go would completely alter your perfect picture of what life should be like.

I know, I know, I shouldn't try to plan my life. I don't know what tomorrow will bring. It's God's will over my own. Have you not picked up that I know this deep in my bones? For the sake of our sanity, can we just agree to take the masks off and admit that we all have a tendency to hold on to what we think life *should* look like? If you're one of the rare unicorns who actually wake up each morning without a clue as to what the day will bring, kudos to you. For the rest of us who need deodorant and concealer, it is incredibly difficult to die to ourselves and stay 100 percent at ease with whatever He intends for us. It's not easy to confidently shout, "But if not, You are still good."

Thankfully, we can find rest in knowing that He is the only one who really knows exactly what we need in our race through this life, and—hallelujah—He is the same one who can give us (and wants to give us) those things. As I sit here and write this, I don't know what God has planned for our family. I don't know if our adventures will be in a branch of the mission field or in a rocking chair at two in the morning, maybe both.

Regardless, I have the peace of the Lord deep in my spirit this afternoon. I smile as I type these words because tiny human or not, God will use this journey of dying to self for His purposes and His glory. He will use me. He will bless me in ways that will fill me to the brim and overflow into the lives around me. He will see me through all of my highs and lows in this life.

Each morning, I have started surrendering my day to Him by intentionally focusing on His will and cultivating my hunger for His heart. I take time to quiet my soul. I look ahead to what is going on that day and identify any areas of control or expectations that may be playing in the background. I pray for protection, begging for Him to replace my mind with His own.

As I type this, it sounds so "holier than thou," but y'all, getting in this habit has been what has freed me from myself. It hasn't been easy. Some days still aren't easy. Sometimes I still cry like a toddler, as I pout and sling things across the room to give them back to Him. Here's the secret, though. Do you know what happens when you don't live every moment with expectations of how life *should* be? You aren't burdened by disappointment, overanalysis, and the compulsive need to control. Do you know what springs forth out of that freedom? Joy—pure, unfiltered, pit-of-your-soul joy. So I am praying that you take my words and experience to heart. I am praying that you recognize your own human nature, lay your picture of a perfect life down, and make it a habit to live each day with zero expectations other than to be completely overcome by His presence and goodness. I pray that His love and peace flow from your life as a continuous, surrendered, joyful "Yes, Lord!"

JACOB

In his younger years, Jacob was the kid from down the street who tricked your younger brother into trading a dollar for two quarters (because obviously two items are better than one). Also, he's a jerk. And his momma? She's the one who helped her kids play pranks, then hid the twerps when their tricks backfired.

I've always known Jacob for a few things—his ladder, wrestling with God, and being a deceiver. I've known him as the character who dreamt of a stairway that extended to heaven and allowed him to see and speak with the Lord. I've known him as the Old Testament dude who wrestled God all night and had his hip knocked out of joint. I knew him as the jerk-face who deceived his dying father and stole his brother's blessing.

It wasn't until I started digging deeper into his story for this book's purposes that I realized what a manipulator and bargainer he really was. There are so many lessons to be learned from Jacob's life, but for the sake of this book, I want to hone in on two specific examples. Before we dive in, it will be helpful to know a little background about our main man, so here's a brief overview:

From Genesis, we learn that Jacob was the son of Isaac and Rebekah. His paternal grandparents were Abraham and Sarah. Can we just pause here and imagine family mealtime?

"Grandpa, tell me a story about your life."

"Well, son, which would you like to hear? The one about how God called me to move away from all I'd ever known? The one where God renamed us and made His covenant with us, telling us that we would be the father and mother of many nations? How about the miraculous story of how your dad was born? Or how about the time we escaped the godless towns just before sulfur rained down from the sky and burned everything up? Not those? Hmm...I know! What about the one where God asked me to sacrifice your dad on the altar? Now that's a good one!"

WHAT? Can you even imagine, y'all?

We are going to pick up Jacob's story in the middle of Genesis 28. By this point, he already has a questionable reputation. He's manipulated his twin brother, Esau, into trading his family birthright for a bowl of stew. (You read that correctly.) Then he teamed with Mommy dear to dress up and deceive his father (who was on his deathbed, might I add) in order to steal Esau's blessing. To throw the cherry on top, Jacob cowardly kissed Momma goodbye and left when he learned how enraged Esau was with the whole ordeal.

When we find him in chapter 28, Jacob is still on the run, traveling to his uncle's house for safety. He has made camp for the night, and the famous dream of Jacob's ladder occurs. Despite the holy terror that Jacob has been, God, being God, honored his stolen blessing. The Lord speaks insight and promise into Jacob's life through this dream.

At the top of the stairway in his dream stood the Lord, and He said, "I am the Lord, the God of your father, Isaac. The ground you are lying on belongs to you. I am giving it to you and your descendants" (Gen. 28:13, NLT).

Can you imagine how unbelievably tired Jacob must have been at this point? He's been traveling with the weight of his past chained to his mind. Though Scripture doesn't tell us if he felt remorse for all he had done, I can only imagine that his heart took a beating. Conniving and stealing from his brother was only the beginning; now his brother wanted him dead. Here comes God, though, promising him that he would have a place to call his and children of his own.

The Lord continued, "Your descendants will be as numerous as the dust of the earth! They will spread out in all directions—to the West and the East, to the North and the South. And all the families of the earth will be blessed through you and your descendants" (Gen. 28:14).

Yes, indeed—Jacob would have descendants!

I found myself wondering how many friends Jacob had at this point in his life. I'm no historian, so I don't know what friendships looked like or if proximity even allowed for friendships outside of family. If so, I can't imagine he was well liked; he was likely known to be deceptive and sly. I surely wouldn't have trusted him! And we already know how his brother felt about him. All that being said, it had to be comforting to know that he wasn't going to always be alone, that someone was going to come eventually and love his ridiculous self. It had to bring him hope, knowing his family would continue to grow for countless generations. That last sentence of verse 14, though. That had to feel redemptive and empowering—to know that even though you've been arrogant and a pain in the rear, God is still going to use YOU and YOUR FAMILY to bless ALL the other families of the earth. It would have left me speechless!

The Lord continued, "What's more, I am with you, and I will protect you wherever you go. One day I will bring you back to this land. I will not leave you until I have finished giving you everything I have promised you" (Gen. 28:15).

As if the promises of family and provision weren't enough, God took the time to reassure Jacob, to speak life into his heart before his next chapter began. He promised to protect him and bring him back to this very spot one day—this intimate, holy spot of vow and hope. Best of all, God promised that he wouldn't leave Jacob's side until these promises were fulfilled.

This is the point where I picture Jacob jumping to his feet, chest out like a peacock, striding forward to his destiny. Confidence is exuding from him, and he grins without fear, knowing the God of his father and grandfather is with him.

He is bold and brave, knowing the Lord will protect him as he continues his journey. He leaves his past behind, accepts who he is called to be, and goes forth as a soldier of the Lord.

If only that was what happened!

I'll give it to him. Jacob did wake and realize that God was with him. He didn't write this dream off as too many cheese curds and crumbs before bed. He even went so far as to turn the rock he'd been using as a pillow into an anointed pillar, naming it Bethel, which means "House of God" (Gen. 28:18–19). When I read this, I was excited. Yes! He's headed in the right direction! You go, boy! Look at you, honoring God!

Then he opened his mouth and proved that he was not only a deceiver but also a manipulator. He was experienced in wheeling and dealing, an if-then kind of man.

Jacob made this vow:

> If God will [one] indeed be with me and pro-
> tect me on this journey, and if [two] He will
> provide me with food and clothing, and if
> [three] I return safely to my father's home,
> then [one] the Lord will certainly be my God.
> And [two] this pillar I have set up will become
> a place for worshiping God, and [three] I will
> present to God a tenth of everything He
> gives me. (Gen. 28:20–22)

I'm not floored at the fact that Jacob has the knee-jerk reaction to be manipulative. After all, he replied to his brother's plea for food by saying that if he sold him the birthright, then he would give him some stew. But Y'ALL, did he really just go there with God? Is he really that audacious?

Jacob listened intently to the Lord's promises of generational land, divine protection and provision, a massive, anointed family, and God's very presence through it all. We know this because he turned right around and used them as bargaining bait. After all these extravagant oaths were made, was Jacob left in awe, praising and trusting the Lord's promises? Did he finally surrender his lonesome journey and vow to obediently follow God? Absolutely not!

He said, "Okay, God. I hear you. I know what you've done in the past. I've seen it! All of those promises sound wonderful. So here's the deal. If you stay true to your word and do one, two, and three, THEN I will surrender everything and do one, two, and three."

What a jerk! I wish I could hear God speak such promises to me! I was so shocked and irritated by his response. I was so disgusted at his lack of appreciation. I was so appalled by the disrespect.

I was *so* Jacob.

There I was, scoffing at good ole Jake while sipping my morning joe. But the reality? I was no better than him. Had I not done the same thing to God? Did I not know how the Lord has provided for and blessed me in the past? Had I not seen it? Did I not know what the Word says—full of promises and truth for my life? Did I not try to make a deal with God? Sure, I didn't audibly bargain with Him, but I also knew that (I can hear my mother say it now) *actions speak louder than words*. Did I not have a quiet, manipulative heart, thinking that if I did everything correctly, the Lord would hold up His end of the bargain and bless us with a baby? I was just a twenty-first-century Jacob, y'all, and I had to be brave enough to call my own bluff.

The Bible tells us, "Above all else, guard your heart, for everything you do flows from it" (Prov. 4:23). Read that last part again. Everything flows from it, because we are emotional beings. Our actions, our thoughts, our words, our motivation— everything is influenced, in some way, by our heartstrings. For me, I was influenced by a deep longing. My actions may have been in line, my thoughts and words may have been obedient, but my *why* was all wrong. I wish I could say it didn't spill into any other areas of my life, but as you'll soon find out, it most certainly did. I'm just a twenty-first-century Jacob.

The deeper I dug into Jacob's story, desperate to find a redemption twist, the more I realized how broken and habitual this man was. I can't imagine what his life would have been like had he not been covered by the generational blessing that began with Abraham years before he was born. It broke my heart to think about it, really. In the same breath, it gave me hope and made my spirit soar. Without Jesus, I'm just a twenty-first-century Jacob.

Tonight, I am humbly reminded of the beauty of radical grace. I'm thankful that I don't have to depend on generational blessings and sacrificial atonement to be made right in the eyes of my God. I'm encouraged by the fact that with each surrender, He "makes us more and more like Him, as we are changed into His glorious image" (2 Cor. 3:18). I'm left awestruck by the precious gift I have in Jesus—that He not only loves and accepts me, as broken as I am, but He holds the power to forgive me and make me new (2 Cor. 5:17).

He alone holds the power to mend my battered heart. He alone can satisfy this yearning in my soul. *Yes, Lord, I believe that You alone can make me whole.*

CONNECT

What sentence, paragraph, or fact from this section stuck with you most? Record it below.

Why could you identify with it? Be specific.

REFLECT

Describe a time where you had expectations of God. Were your expectations met? If so, how does that impact your surrender today? If not, how did you respond to these unmet expectations (think emotions, actions, mindset, etc.)?

Are there any current areas in which you are striving to trust the Lord but still expecting specific solutions/answers from Him?

RESPOND

PRAISE: Name four specific praises of His past provisions/answers/solutions in your life.

1.

2.

3.

4.

REPENT: Name three expectations you have had/currently have of God, even if they were unintentional.

1.

2.

3.

ASK: Name two situations in which you need the Lord to change your perspective, in regard to your expectations.

1.

2.

YES, LORD: Pick one of the above situations. What do you need to actively practice in order to begin making the shift from expectation to surrender?

1.

CLING TO SCRIPTURE

Submit yourselves, then, to God. Resist the devil, and he will flee from you. (James 4:7)

My son, give me your heart and let your eyes delight in my ways. (Proverbs 23:26)

Those who know your name trust in you, for you, Lord have never forsaken those who seek you. (Psalm 9:10)

Which verse did you choose to commit to memory and utilize as you learn to accept the Lord's will over your own? Record it below.

Battle III:
Fair Vs. Fear

JOYFUL JEALOUSY

I was sitting at lunch with my teaching team when it happened. She bounced over to our table with a grin that spread from ear to ear.

"I'm pregnant," she squealed and giggled.

She was beaming, the purest joy dancing in her eyes! Without a second thought, I leapt off my seat and threw my arms around her neck with excitement. What a blessing! The world was going to gain a miniature version of this sweet soul who always smiled and offered a kind word to those around her. That, my friends, is something worth celebrating! After the hugging and sharing of details ended, she gathered her class and headed back to her room with a giddy pep in her step. As the door closed behind them, my adrenaline settled, my mind wandered, and my heart sank.

She and her husband had started trying about the same time Brock and I did. It was month four at this point, and she was already three months along, meaning they ended up being one of the handful of couples who experience the blessing of pregnancy the first or second month they try. I felt discouraged and frustrated. While her body was busy growing a baby, mine was still off-roading and refusing to establish a normal pattern. Within the next two weeks, I would take my fourth negative test. I would also celebrate the birth of three of my friends' precious little ones whom I love very, very much.

When I closed my car door and headed home that afternoon, I cried. My mind had been distracted by jealousy for the entire second half of my day. I had been dwelling on the fact that we didn't have news to share yet. It's never a good thing to dwell on negative thoughts and emotions. It left me in a sour mood and with an entitled perspective. As I drove and my heart screamed even louder, I was flooded with reasons this wasn't fair.

Wasn't I the one who had been told from a very young age, "You're going to make an amazing mom one day, kid?" Was I not the one whom people continuously said had a natural instinct with kids of all ages, both in and out of a teaching environment? Was my husband not the one whom kids flock to when he's around because of the joy and love he shows them? Were we not the couple whom people always smiled at and told, "I can't wait to see y'all as parents—you're going to be incredible"? Were we not the ones who worked for five years to prepare ourselves and our home to be the best it could be before trying to bring a small soul into the world? *Why not us?*

I didn't know it was possible to feel such joy and such jealousy at the same time. How can half of my heart want to celebrate with excitement and the other half want to roll my eyes and scoff? It sounds so ridiculous to put words to the battle in my mind and heart. We were four months in, for crying out loud! Not years—months. My friend and her husband were the anomaly in this story, not us. Our experience was considered normal at this point in our journey. All rationality aside, I can pinpoint these few weeks as the first time my faith in the Lord's timing took a huge hit. After a long run and a cup of hot coffee, my mind cleared, and the cry of "It's not fair" was drowned out by my joy for these women in my life. My heart was immensely thankful for these four healthy babies and their mommas who were thriving. What a gift for us all!

You know, the enemy made a great point, though. Yes, these four stories aren't a reason to pout about fairness, but do you know what is? Pregnancies of women who are infuriated with a positive—those who don't want their child. Women who bring children into this world and refuse to take care of them for one reason or another. Women who aren't even trying to have children and view their child as an "oops" or a "mistake." How in the world have Brock and I been tracking, trying, learning, and preparing, all to no avail, but women who aren't interested turn up pregnant as easily as catching a common cold?

Yes, THAT was what was not fair. Just thinking about it made my heart bitter and my blood boil. In true mature-adult fashion, I started throwing an emotional toddler tantrum with God. I wanted Him to know how angry and upset I was with this fact of life. I wanted Him to see how badly I was hurting. I wanted Him to know how mad I was at Him. In the midst of my tantrum, a toxic whisper entered my mind and began to grow louder.

"It's not going to happen. You two are doing everything right. If it was going to happen, it would have already, what with everything you're doing. You're obviously not meant to be parents. Chin up. You gave it your best. It just isn't in the will. Let it go, and find another dream to dream. Maybe your friends will let you love on their kids some."

I absorbed the words and panicked. My heart began asking all the wrong questions. What if this isn't God's will at all? What if we're trying in vain, going through heartbreak after heartbreak to simply dig ourselves deeper into hopelessness? Does our story end here because no one will be alive to carry on our name, our legacy? Will we lose our friends as their families grow and we're still just the two of us? Is something wrong with our health that we are unaware of? Is Brock going to be so disappointed in me that it will drive our marriage into the ground?

The more I panicked, the more I spiraled and sunk. With each passing month, negative test, and pregnancy announcement by those around me, I felt like I was slowly losing control of my heart. It wasn't fun, and it wasn't fair. It also wasn't Jesus.

One of my favorite personal mantras comes from Tony Evans's book, *Kingdom Woman*, where he discusses the woman in the Bible who had been bent over for eighteen years.[2] He points out that while everyone else had addressed the fruit of the problem (her outward symptom), Jesus addressed the root of the problem (the underlying cause), which was spiritual bondage. Addressing the root of the issue is what set the woman free. From Pastor Evans's teaching, my mantra of "Pray for the root, not the fruit" was born, and I use it to keep my heart in check quite often.

So let's do it. Let's call to light the root of my problem, shall we? Though jealousy was the fruit on display, it wasn't the root of the issue. What was causing the jealousy? The stealthy snare laid by the enemy to take me captive was none other than the spirit of fear and its right-hand man, the thief of comparison. They are a team that can take up residence in our lives and wreak havoc before we even realize they're there. Their handiwork can manifest differently in each person. For me, fear and comparison were shining brightly through my envy.

Fear and jealousy create such a vicious cycle. Underlying fear causes jealousy to stir. When we allow our thoughts to dwell on this jealousy, it causes our fear to intensify. What if we never get that thing we long for that everyone else seems to have? Those fearful thoughts cause jealousy to grow, which leads to greater fear; it goes on and on and on. Eventually, this cycle has the potential to create other spin-off storms in your soul, such as bitterness, isolation, and depression. It's hard to believe that such a winding path of destruction can result from one attribute, one habit in your life. But that's how Satan works—weighing you down a little at a time so that he won't give himself away until one day you're being crushed by life, wondering how you even got there. Enough. It's time to deal with the root. (You still listening, Jenna? Just checking.)

---

[2] Tony Evans and Chrystal E. Hurst, *Kingdom Woman: Embracing Your Purpose, Power, and Possibilities* (Carol Stream: Tyndale House Publishers, 2015), Page 48.

It seems so simple, almost too simple. We understand Satan wants to steal our joy, but do we understand he wants to blur our focus? We know Satan craves to see chaos in our lives, but do we see his schemes to birth discord in our relationships by using our family and friends against us (or us against them)? We know he would give anything to make us doubt God and His perfect will for our lives, but do we recognize the decoys of comparison and jealousy when they surface? Do we recognize that it's all part of his battle strategy to distract us in our pain until we're stuck in an endless cycle of shallow surrender? Take our eyes off the cross? Do we realize we have a death grip on our heartache while he has a death grip on our heart?

How often do we do this to God? How often do we use the same breath to praise His goodness and scream that He isn't being fair? How often do we pray for a blessing, only to turn around and pout that it isn't what we wanted? How often do we panic and cry out, then refuse to let Him take control? I know I can't be the only one who has orally surrendered to Him without any actions to back it up.

I heard my beautiful friend Laura's words when she reassured me that my story was being masterfully written even in this season of waiting. I was listening when she reassured me that the blessing at the end of the journey was going to be far greater and more beautiful than I could ever imagine, whatever it may be and however long it may take. I clung to the truth that the Lord hadn't forgotten the desire He gave me, that He had a purpose in calling me to walk this path. I heard her when she challenged me to be still and see how He may be working behind the scenes in the midst of this.

I still didn't want to hear it. Though she spoke a gentle truth that my heart needed to hear, I still felt broken. At this point, I had not arrived at my crossroads of surrender, so my hope was taking a beating while I plastered a grin on my face. She knew this, and I praise God for her boldness and immense love for me. She loved me far too much to tell me what I want to hear. She tenderly reminded me that I could choose which emotions to feed in my heart and mind. True, my natural, flesh-driven reactions may always be jealousy and fear, but I could choose what to do with them. I could let them fester and paralyze me, or I could choose to transform them into praise. It sounds so cliché, I know. I wanted to roll my eyes at her too.

Girl, you don't have to tell me. Praising when you're angry or hurt is so much harder than people give it credit for. We challenge each other to praise through the storms like it's as easy as picking which color nail polish you want on your toes—it's not. Don't fall for Satan's trap, though. If praise were solely based on how we feel, it would merely be celebration. If the goodness and worthiness of God was based on our satisfaction, it would mean His aim is to simply earn our approval. Sure, we praise Him *when* we're thankful, but that is not *why* we praise Him. We praise Him because He is God. We praise Him because He is good. We praise Him because, for some reason, He sees our shattered souls as treasures and wants nothing more than to wrap us in His everlasting love.

If I'm being completely transparent, praising through the struggle can be a mere act of obedience sometimes. At least it was for me. Nevertheless, I praised.

"Even though I don't understand, I will praise You.

"Even though my heart is longing and torn, I will praise You.

"Even though my flesh cries out for fairness, I will praise You.

"Even though my soul is tired and my mind is angry, I will praise You.

"I will praise You, not because You will give me what I want if I do, but because You are who you say You are. You are unwavering. You are Truth. You see my life from beginning to end, and You know things to come that aren't on my radar. You know what I need, not just what I want. You cry when I cry. You hurt when I hurt. You have not forsaken my heart, despite the lies the enemy whispers. I will praise you because even if the earthly gift doesn't come, I have already received the priceless reward—I am Yours. And even though there are days that my heart screams that it isn't enough, my soul is calmed by the reassurance that it is."

Jesus will always, always be enough.

It's funny—when you go against your flesh and sprint to the cross in obedience, there is no power in hell that can stop you. When you take back your focus and fixate on the only thing that truly matters, Satan's grip on your soul weakens. When you desperately free-fall into the arms of your Savior, you discover the quiet oasis in the storm. You find peace, joy, and the confidence to once again shout, "Yes, Lord!"

RACHEL

We've all been there before—the place where you are desperately longing for something. We convince ourselves that we won't be fulfilled without it. We persuade ourselves into believing that our worth is riding on it. We notice how so many others seem to have that one thing, whatever it may be, and it stirs jealousy in our spirit. We want to stomp our feet and throw a hissy fit in protest.

This is exactly what I visualize when I think about Rachel. No, I'm not referring to Rachel Green, the beloved *Friends* character. Though, now that I think about it, it does sound like her sassy self, doesn't it? The Rachel I'm referring to is the woman in the Bible found in Genesis. She is often known for her jealousy, which is how she landed the leading role in this chapter.

Rachel was the younger daughter of Laban, the uncle who took Jacob in after his parents sent him away. Genesis 29:17 tells us that she had a "beautiful figure and a lovely face." She was so beautiful that Jacob quickly fell in love with her and agreed to work for seven years to pay for Rachel's hand in marriage. Seven years of labor may seem like a long time and a hefty price, but when we keep reading, the Word tells us that "[Jacob's] love for her was so strong that it seemed to him but a few days" (Gen. 29:20). Dude had it bad, y'all!

After his seven years were completed, Laban agreed to give Jacob his daughter's hand in marriage. On their wedding night, however, Laban veiled Leah, Rachel's older sister, and took her to Jacob instead. (Please don't let it be lost to you that Jacob, the man who disguised himself to steal his

66

brother's blessing, has now had his promised wife stolen and exchanged for her sister in disguise.) When Jacob realized it was Leah the next morning, he was infuriated. Laban ended up weaseling another seven years of labor out of Jacob in exchange for Rachel's hand as well. Laban gave Rachel to him upfront this time, and Jacob "loved her much more than Leah" (Gen. 29:30).

I know, none of this screams jealousy, does it? I feel like all this background information is necessary to set the stage, though. Imagine how great Rachel must feel. This man is completely captivated by her beautiful self, so much so that he worked seven years to earn her hand in marriage. When he was given her sister instead, it was not enough. He loved Rachel so much that he vowed to work another seven years just to be able to call her his bride. She was the favorite. She was Jacob's heartbeat.

It doesn't say, but I'm sure this had to inflate Rachel's ego, at least to some degree. I don't know what her relationship with Leah was like before all this went down, but I can only imagine that this caused some discord in their relationship afterward. It's not a stretch to think it may have caused her to look down and internally (maybe even externally) stick her tongue out at her big sis. "He loves me more! He loves me more!"

Let's keep going.

"When the Lord saw that Leah was unloved, he enabled her to have children, but Rachel could not conceive" (Gen. 29:31). It doesn't say why Rachel couldn't conceive. It just says she couldn't, and oh man, was she fit to be tied because of it! After Leah gave birth to her fourth child, Rachel became green with envy and went into full drama-queen mode. Genesis 30:1 tells us that she begged Jacob by saying, "Give me children, or I'll die!"

At this point in the story, I tried to picture how Brock would respond if I did this to him. I can just see us sitting at the dinner table, me in tears, throwing this out in a desperate attempt to communicate my longing. Girl, it would break his heart! I can hear him now saying, "Woman!" (That's how I know I've hit a nerve!) I know for a fact it would hurt him to see me wrestling with such heartache. But if I were actually outrageous enough to propose that he had the power to magically grant me my wish and was withholding it, he would be crushed and infuriated.

It's no wonder Jacob responds to her by saying, "Am I God? He's the one who has kept you from having children" (Gen. 30:2). Now you would think that after such a dramatic display and being reminded that only God has the power to grant this gift, she would apologize for being such a brat and start praying about the situation. Instead, Rachel did what so many of us are guilty of doing—she conjured a human solution for her problem. She replied to Jacob's reprimand by saying, "Take my maid, Bilah, and sleep with her. She will bear children for me, and through her, I can have a family, too" (Gen. 30:3). What?

First, poor Bilah. Can you imagine being owned by another woman and being told to sleep with her husband? Can you imagine having to carry and give birth to your child, knowing he wouldn't be yours in the end? Can you even imagine? Second, Rachel is nuts—plain and simple. She claimed Bilah's son as her own and named him Dan which, according to the ESV Study Bible, means "judge." Do you know why she chose Dan? "She said, 'God has vindicated me'" (Gen. 30:6). Oh, the fun doesn't stop there, girl! Bilah gave birth to a second child, whom Rachel also took and named Naphtali, which means "wrestle," according to the same study bible. Why this name? "For she said, 'I have struggled hard with my sister, and I'm winning!'" (Gen. 30:8). Notice she didn't rejoice at having tiny toes to kiss, a little one to love. No, she's celebrating that she's winning (face-palm). Is this even about having her own children anymore?

Never mind the fact that Rachel has always held the highest position in Jacob's heart and is surrounded by a family full of loved ones. Never mind that Jacob has always been infatuated with her, while her sister has been yearning for his love and approval, hoping that with each child, she will finally gain it (Gen. 29:32, 34). Poor Leah, right? I know, girl. I was so rooting for the underdog in this story. Rise up and become a beautiful butterfly, Leah, and stick it to your crazy sister!

Nope. Not to be outdone by her little sis, Leah jumped on the bandwagon and played the same childish game (pun intended). She gave her maid, Zilpah, to Jacob. In turn, Leah added two more sons to her count. She also had two more biological sons and a daughter. Leah proclaimed, "Now my husband will treat me with respect, for I have given him six sons" (Gen. 30:20). Bless her heart.

I'm super glad Jacob had so many sons to pal with, though, because the level of estrogen in this story gives me hives! The fact that a woman's value in that day rode on her ability to have children probably only intensified the hormonal hissy fits. I do have to admit, though, I still feel bad for Leah. It has to be tough to be thrown into a life you didn't choose, only to constantly be undervalued and unloved no matter what you do.

Regardless, can we take a deep breath, shake our noggin to refocus, and realize how toxic jealousy and comparison became in these women's lives? Can you imagine the tension in their family? Can you imagine the stress Jacob must have felt with his family constantly feuding?

Just for kicks and giggles, let's play with an alternate ending.

Let's pretend that Rachel didn't go bonkers and just trusted the Lord. Yes, her heart did still hurt and long, but she didn't let those emotions take control. Because Leah loved her sister and saw her struggle, she was there as solitude and a place of rest when Rachel's emotions tried to get the best of her. Since Rachel had such a strong relationship with Leah, she also had a strong bond with her nephews and nieces. Jacob saw how the two women cared for each other, how his family functioned in harmony, and his heart softened toward Leah. It was a serene life. Then when Rachel became pregnant, everyone shed tears of joy, instead of sighs of relief that the madness might actually be coming to an end.

Because Rachel did end up conceiving. Genesis 30:22 says, "Then God remembered Rachel's plight and answered her prayers by enabling her to have children." She gave birth to Joseph, who would grow up to be one of the most prominent archetypes of Jesus in the Bible.

Unfortunately, our alternate ending wasn't this family's reality. Though Rachel did finally give birth to a great man of God, it probably wasn't into a warm and peaceful environment. The Bible doesn't say, but again, if I had to guess, I would think Rachel would have some regrets about how she treated Jacob and her sister. Instead of having a unified home, full of love and support, her jealousy stirred up an environment of competition, comparison, and tension. Even if Rachel was full of remorse and apologized, I wonder how easily their deep wounds healed. I wonder if they reconciled and moved forward, leaving it all in the past. I wonder if they even wanted to.

Friend, I don't know what your heart is yearning for. I don't know how long your wait has been. I don't know what stories of triumph and heartbreak have peppered your journey thus far. What I do know is that waiting is hard. I know that watching others celebrate the blessing you hope for can be painful. Trusting the Lord can seem impossible some days. I don't, for one minute, downplay the battle that rages in your soul because of it.

I do, however, plead with you to take hold of jealousy when it rears its ugly head. I beg you to do whatever it takes to break the habit of comparison. I don't know what that will mean or look like for your life, but whatever it may be, I pray you make it a priority. Rachel's story is just one of many throughout history that display just how venomous envy can be to your heart and mind. We've seen how envy has the potential to spill over and pollute your relationships, your home, and your life.

I pray you recognize the enemy's tactics, call them to the light, and praise the Lord boldly through the tears. Scripture is clear that when we submit to God and resist the temptations we're faced with, the enemy will flee from us (James 4:7). It goes on to reassure us that when we draw near to God, He responds by drawing near to us (James 4:8). This is a beautiful place to be because it is exactly where we find the peace that surpasses all our human understanding—the peace that guards our minds and hearts in this war for our life (Phil. 4:7).

The enemy wants you to think it's too simple, too cliché, that all this talk of drawing near to and worshiping Jesus won't actually free you from this habit of comparing and the jealousy that comes with it.

I dare you to prove him wrong.

I double dog dare you to take hold of your mind and heart, throw your head back, and praise.

Yes, Lord, I will choose to praise.

CONNECT

What sentence, paragraph, or fact from this section stuck with you most? Record it below.

Why could you identify with it? Be specific.

REFLECT

Think of a time when have you experienced jealousy, even just internally? Maybe you're experiencing it in your current season of life.

How did/does that jealousy alter your day-to-day life? (Emotions, relationships, routines, hobbies, etc.)

RESPOND

PRAISE. Name four specific praises for others you know who already have what you're waiting/praying for.

1.

2.

3.

4.

REPENT. Name three ways you've allowed jealousy, comparison, or anger to reign free in your heart, instead of making those thoughts obedient to Christ.

1.

2.

3.

ASK. Name two situations where you can anticipate those emotions rising again, and ask God to prepare you to meet them with grace, peace, and humble joy.

1.

2.

YES, LORD. Name one realistic step you can take today to replace jealousy with joy.

    1.

CLING TO SCRIPTURE

Love is patient, love is kind. It does not envy, it does not boast, it is not proud. (1 Corinthians 13:4)

A heart at peace gives life to the body, but envy rots the bones. (Proverbs 14:30)

Do not be overcome by evil, but overcome evil with good. (Romans 12:21)

Which verse did you choose to commit to memory and utilize as you learn to replace jealousy and comparison with truth? Record it below.

Battle IV:
Controlled Chaos

PUZZLED PEACE

When I think of how far we, as a society, have come in our knowledge of all things, especially in the world of science, it amazes me. The leaps and bounds we've taken to further our understanding about the world around us, even just in my lifetime, often leaves me dumbfounded.

When we embarked on this quest to grow our family, I confided in one of my coworkers and friends who had just welcomed her first child into the world seven months earlier. I shared my concerns and fears. As she was giving me advice and throwing around all the fertility buzzwords, she quickly realized how little I actually knew about this whole process other than the "baby dance" part. She showed me an app that would help me track all of my fertility data and learn as I go. There truly is an app for everything, y'all! I quickly discovered that all things—from cervical details and mood swings to basal body temperature and other physical symptoms—could be telltale clues of which phase of my cycle I was in. Who knew? (Obviously, not me.)

Data has always fascinated me. Whether I am studying my students' progress in the classroom or researching topics of interest, analyzing numbers and finding trends has always been a guilty pleasure of mine. Needless to say, I quickly fell in love with logging my fertility data into the app. When I logged new information, it would give me insight and facts related to what I logged. These led me to further research about female hormones, holistic tips, different symptoms, the root cause of those symptoms, others' experiences, on and on and on.

This was all especially intriguing to me in the beginning because my body was completely out of rhythm in regard to my cycle. The length varied by ten or more days each time, all of which fell into the "irregular" category. My symptoms were sporadic, never showing any of the trends I so eagerly anticipated. At first, this left me extremely frustrated and discouraged. Not to be defeated, I resolved to choose optimism, keep logging and learning, and wait patiently for my body to find its groove.

By the third month of data tracking and research, I knew what prescription options were available to make my body function normally should we ever need them. I also knew which essential oils, supplements, teas, foods, and physical activities had positive and negative impacts on fertility. I knew which specific resources would be helpful leading up to ovulation. I knew what to change in my routine, post ovulation, in case conception had occurred. I knew in which phases of my cycle I should get the most exercise, expect more fatigue, and avoid extremely hot baths.

This was all very useful, but my body still didn't have an established pattern. I never really knew which phase of my cycle I was experiencing or when ovulation actually occurred, so sticking to the tricks was, well, tricky. This brought a whole new level of confusion. Nevertheless, I continued to swallow the hesitancy and frustration; I was insistent on pushing through with my hopeful attitude and arsenal of new-found knowledge.

By month seven, I was sitting across from Laura during our coffee date and unloading my defeated heart of anger and confusion. I was so fed up with all of it. I had spent months carefully controlling all the external factors in my life. What I ate, drank, supplemented, and avoided was meticulously considered and planned out. I was ridiculously diligent to keep a steady exercise routine and sleep pattern. Though I did notice some positive changes, my body was still all over the place. I mean, I know I've always had a natural stubborn streak, but

REALLY? Y'ALL! The fact that I couldn't get myself together frustrated me immensely.

"Girl, you are so stressed," Laura whispered lovingly, as she tried to calm my raging heart.

After a good, long eye roll, I fired back at her, "I'm not stressed! In fact, I've gone above and beyond to AVOID stress for the past seven months." *She's been there for literally every day of it! She should know!* I was well aware of the detrimental impact stress could inflict on all areas of my health, especially fertility. Obviously, I wasn't going to let that be what stood in my way.

As she sat there and stared at me, I shifted uncomfortably and laughed. I calmly clarified that I was busy, but I wasn't stressed. I was happy at home. I was in a sweet place at work. I was excited and motivated at church. Yes, I had a lot to do, but it was everything I thoroughly enjoyed doing. None of it felt like a chore or busied me to the point that I was losing sleep or altering my routine. If anything, I was exercising and sleeping more consistently than I had in quite a while! So no, bestie, I wasn't stressed.

Y'all, I will say this a hundred times by the end of the book. I'm sure you'll end up thinking, "Geez, woman, you sound like a broken record!" I assure you the repetition is intentional because it is so important. If you don't have a friend who will smile at you with patience and love, listen with compassion, and then call your bluff, one who will hold your stubborn self accountable and lead you back to Jesus, you need to find one.

As I continued to defend myself, Laura lovingly listened, understood my heart, and stood as a safe place for me to express my raw emotions. When I finished explaining how insanely unfair it all was, she picked me right up out of my righteous wallowing and spoke truth into my life.

"Jenna, I love you, and I hear you. You may not be physically stressed, but, sister, you are mentally and emotionally spent. I know you don't want to hear this, and you're a big girl and can take care of yourself. It's your choice, but I think it would be wise to stop logging your data and researching it all. It's making you nuts."

I clutched my pearls and gasped, glaring at her in horror. Such foul language! *Stop logging my data? Stop trying my holistic tips and tricks? Was she crazy?* God had given me these gifts to utilize and she wants me to consider abandoning them? I had a seven-month streak going at this point. I couldn't just stop! What if this is the month when all the pieces would finally come together? When I eventually realized she wasn't going to apologize for offending my dedicated heart, nor was she going to try to explain herself, I quieted my ego and ate my humble pie.

As much as I wanted to stab her hand with my cake pop stick, I knew I had to take her advice to heart. I had been blessed with a sister-friend who offered wise counsel and steady accountability with grace and love. And she was speaking the truth—God had given me this awesome tool to help me learn during the trial and error of the baby game, and I had allowed Satan to corrupt it with my flesh-driven desire to control. Let's face it, I wasn't just learning anymore. My sole intent behind all of it was to bring forth MY desired outcome in MY time. When MY expectations weren't met, I allowed it to justify my anger with the situation. It made me want to stomp my feet at God. I was doing everything in MY power, after all. Where was HE at? (Bless my little heart!)

I quietly sat and digested the truth of Laura's words. She confirmed what I honestly knew but had been avoiding—I had lost myself in my desperation to "fix me." I had spent months trying to execute every tip and trick, convinced that if I didn't, our dream would die. Trapped in this exhausting carousel, I knew the only way to find the peace I so desperately craved was to give this battle back to the Lord. Even though my heart was crying out in protest, I knew I needed to trust that in His perfect time, He would put my body in proper working order. And as surprising as it may be, y'all, He didn't need my help to do it.

I locked eyes with my friend, and I felt the weight of her challenge. The research, tips and tricks, and constant data-logging had to stop. In order to make room for the peace of Christ to rule in my heart once again (Col. 3:15), I had to relinquish my perceived control. She praised God for my willingness to surrender and helped me craft a practical battle plan of obedience. I praised Him for her boldness and undaunted love.

A week later, I sat confused. "Where's the peace at, Jesus?" Though I had not acted on it, I was still burning with the need to complete my daily list of fertility tricks. I was starting to lose sleep, and I felt my anxiety starting to spike. What if Laura was wrong? What if this urge is really the Lord pressing me to continue on so He can finally make the pieces fall into place?

My throat caught as it hit me. This need to perform my fertility to-do list was not prompted by the Holy Spirit. No, it was a compulsion. All these tips and tricks had morphed into compulsions, rooted in my old, annoying companion—OCD. How did I miss that?

What you probably don't know about me—and what I honestly hesitated to share—is that since I was young, I have battled obsessive compulsive disorder (OCD). I'm not referring to the nonchalant label society has adopted for clean and organized people. I'm referring to the mental chaos where thoughts spiral out of control, become obsessions, and threaten to take hold of one's life through incessant compulsions.

The majority of my first twenty years of life were held captive by it. When I was young, my mother noticed this "quirk," as I so lovingly call it. She saw my fears manifest in compulsions that I had to complete to ward off the tragedy that I was certain would strike if I didn't. Paired with my innate need to be scheduled and have a routine, OCD caused a lot of stress for both of us while I was growing up. It must have been tough for my sweet mama trying to distinguish between my strong-willed personality and my compulsions. Watching me buzz around and helplessly obsess had to break her heart. I still sit in awe of what a good mom I have, y'all. I always joke that she has earned extra crowns in heaven for raising me, but I say that with a large degree of seriousness.

I could write pages of examples of all the ways my obsessive thoughts have manifested in compulsive routines and heartbreak throughout my life. Praise God, He has healed it, for the most part, in my adult years. I've now trained myself to recognize them when they surface. Over time, I've become skilled at taking them captive and battling them with scripture, logic, and strategy.

That's why I was left panicked and speechless when I realized this whole struggle was actually a subtle sabotage from the enemy, rooted in OCD. No wonder I wasn't flooded with the peace that surpasses all understanding; I had tried suppressing compulsions without addressing the fear that birthed them, though I wasn't exactly sure what that fear was. Knowing it had to be unearthed, I quieted my soul and carefully guided my mind down the winding rabbit hole my heart had unknowingly created.

Okay, Jenna, what's the worst that would happen if your body didn't regulate and find its groove? Well, we wouldn't have kids, and it would be my fault. → That would crush Brock. → The Oakes name would die with us since he's the only male that can continue it. → Then he would resent me for that, even if he says he wouldn't. → Slowly, it would drive us apart. → Our marriage would eventually end. → He'd find someone else who could give him the gift I was supposed to give him.

Oh my! *That's* why I had this incessant urge to do everything in my power to improve our chances. The enemy had taken my fear of not figuring my body out and ran with it. He convinced me that if I didn't do my part, God wouldn't bless our family. *That's* why I couldn't miss a day of performing every trick I had learned and why I had developed a lengthy nighttime routine to complete. *That's* why, even though I felt compelled to keep track of everything, I hated it. *That's* why I felt anger and resentment instead of peace and hope.

I know it all sounds ridiculously dramatic. Spiraled fears within OCD are rarely logical, if ever. Those who battle them usually know this, and it frustrates us greatly. We want desperately to brush the fears and compulsions off. It all ends up being more irritating than soothing because we hate how we have to complete them. When this is a hidden secret of your story, it's so easy for the enemy to enslave you in the lie that something is terribly wrong with you. That lie can take you down a dark road if you're not careful. It's why it is so very important to be able to recognize and take captive our fears, then combat them with scripture and truth, even when it seems impossible.

The TRUTH is that my God has told me He knew me before I was even a thought in my parents' mind (Jer. 1:5). He has had all my days planned since before I was born (Ps. 139:16). He assures me that there is a specific time for everything (Eccles. 3.1). I shouldn't rely on my own knowledge of how things work (Prov. 23:4) because nothing can change God's will for my life (Isa. 14:27). He will never fail or abandon me (Heb. 13:5).

I don't know your hidden battles. I don't know the lies Satan whispers in your mind or the fears he tries to disguise as your reality. What I do know is that we all have them. We all so desperately want to believe that if we just put forth enough effort, we may be able to avoid the worst. At the very least, we remain confident that God will honor our efforts; maybe we won't ever experience our deepest desire, but surely He'll keep the worst from happening. *Surely.*

Oh, sister, I love your passion, your dedication to what you love. How terribly tragic that the enemy would use it to paralyze you! It's one of his most notorious schemes, though—to keep us focused on what we fear will happen, instead of battling against the spirit of fear, itself.

Let's call Satan's conniving tail out, shall we? Let's call him out and name the chaos he causes in our hearts. Let's choose to shine a light on his dark, manipulative attempts to wreak havoc in our lives. And, friend, if you are battling quietly behind that beautiful lipsticked smile, resolve to throw pride out the door and let others in on your war. Let them pull you out of isolation and be prayer warriors in your life.

Satan loves an isolated soul.

Satan loves a confused mind.

Satan loves a doubtful heart.

Satan loves chaos.

Not today, Satan.

My soul has such peace knowing that I don't have to figure out the details, even when my flesh screams otherwise. I feel encouraged when I remember that God's will isn't riding on my shoulders. I feel empowered to know that my life is so valuable to the Lord that Satan feels the need to stir doubt in my soul. His plans are so good, His timing so perfect, that the enemy feels the need to do whatever is necessary to hinder my pursuit of freedom in Jesus. True, my soul still feels the need to worry, to wonder, to control. But now when I hear the subtle, urgent lie that I have to do something, I hear the lion in my spirit roar louder, **"It's already done, beloved. Will you trust me?"**

Yes, Lord. I will choose to trust You.

SAUL

When Brock was a sophomore in college, his heart started longing for his future bride, though we were still a few years from meeting. He became laser-focused on what was to come and how to best prepare for his family one day. He started viewing career options through a different lens, keeping his eyes open for his bride and praying for the Lord to prepare them both for the day they would finally meet. At a church service that September, God put a word on his pastor's heart for him, "You will have the perfect bride at the perfect time."

Soon after this happened, he went back to his home and wrote a letter to his future wife, detailing what had happened, where his heart currently was, and how he was praying over her. Years later, I now keep the letter in my Bible as a special treasure, and each time I read it, it makes my heart smile. Though he kept it hidden until we were married, he shared this story with me about a year into our relationship. Looking back, I'm sure he meant it as a romantic gesture, but it made me panic! What did he mean "the perfect bride"?

You better believe that I was hyper aware of every word, action, and Cheeto-breath kiss after that! At this point, we were both pretty sure of where our relationship was headed, and it was exciting to think about our future. (Well, until I remembered I was supposed to be the "perfect bride"). What would he think if he knew I woke up with dragon's breath, looking like my cat had sucked on my hair while I slept? Totally frantic, I started going out of my way to present myself as the version of "perfect" that I believed he would love.

About two weeks later, Brock looked at me and cautiously asked, "What's up with you lately? Are you okay?" By the end of our conversation, all of the cards were on the table, and Brock had dragged my tail back to the cross once more. I still remember his face when I told him what had been running through my mind. He scrunched his nose, pursed his lips, and said, "He already brought us together. If you're supposed to be my bride, you'll be perfect because God made you to be. Not because of all of this...stuff...that you think you need to do. You need to relax and trust Him." Relax and trust? Did he know who I was?

How often do we meet the restlessness of the unknown with a thirst for resolution? How often does our heart whisper, "You're running out of time!" We feel God working in our lives and have faith that His sovereign plan is good; we know this promised truth deep in our bones. Nevertheless, we begin to feel weary and worn as the enemy taunts us with the endless possibilities that loom ahead. Convincing ourselves, we press forward in haste, intent on staying one step ahead.

Saul was no different. Though fully intending to honor the Lord as he led his troops, he acted in foolish haste. Though his inner dialogue convinced him that he was fulfilling the Lord's calling as king, Saul's outer dialogue gave his heart's true focus away.

We are first introduced to the tall and handsome man named Saul in 1 Samuel 9. His father's donkeys had wandered off, and Saul was sent to retrieve them. A servant was instructed to join him, and the pair set off to bring the herd home. After searching for days, Saul convinced himself it would be best to give up the quest. Thankfully, his servant urged him to put in one last-ditch effort—to seek help from Samuel, the Godly prophet who lived nearby.

What they didn't know is that the day before, the Lord told Samuel, "About this time tomorrow, I will send you a man from the land of Benjamin. Anoint him to be the leader of my people, Israel. He will rescue them from the Philistines"

(1 Sam. 9:15–16). As Saul approached him, Samuel heard the Lord whisper, "That's the man I told you about! He will rule my people" (1 Sam. 9:17).

Wow! Do you realize what just happened? This guy went out to rescue donkeys, and he came home as the appointed king of Israel! Needless to say, Saul stepped into his kingship knowing the Lord was with him. He knew he was called, and he was confident in the Lord's plans for his life. However, as we see in the following chapters, that didn't stifle his innate, human tendencies.

In 1 Samuel 13, we find Saul leading the Israelite army well and defeating the Philistines, one garrison at a time. As you can imagine, this news spread like wildfire and enraged the remaining Philistine troops. 1 Samuel 13:4–5 tells us, "The Philistines now hated the Israelites more than ever. [They] mustered a mighty army of 3,000 chariots, 6,000 charioteers, and as many warriors as the grains of sand on the seashore."

The Israelite army could feel the enemy's pressure, and they trembled with fear. Instead of being instructed to advance on the fast-approaching enemy, they were instructed by Saul to take heart and wait. The prophet Samuel had not yet arrived to sacrifice the required burnt offerings, and the Lord would not bless their coming battle until he had done so. As the weight of the unknown bared down, his troops hid and tried to escape. Though his mighty army slowly dwindled, Saul continued to obediently wait and wait and wait.

After all, he knew the Lord had already proclaimed their victory over the enemy. It had all been ordained ahead of time. He had been anointed as the Israelite's leader by God Himself. Still, he was human and had been waiting for a solid week for Samuel, who was still nowhere to be found. Saul continued to see his troops fade, and it made his little heart panic. Their adversary was waiting like a prowling lion, eager to issue their attack at any moment. He had to do something.

Unwilling to delay the battle any longer, Saul decided to use his God-given mind to take matters into his own hands.

Though the Lord had not permitted him to do so, Saul "sacrificed [the offerings] himself" (1 Sam. 13: 9).

I want to pause here and consider the emotions he may have been feeling in this moment. His inner dialogue probably sounded like that of a child trying to elude his parents: "I know they said not to, but I'll get it done quickly. I'll prove I can do it. They may be a little mad that I didn't listen, but they'll also be so proud of the result!" As their leader, he decided to do what he felt needed to be done. The Lord did appoint him to lead well, after all. Surely, He didn't expect them to remain sitting ducks and be destroyed.

"Just as Saul was finishing with the burnt offering, Samuel arrived. Saul went out to meet and welcome him, but Samuel said, 'What is this you have done?'" (1 Sam. 13:11). Uh-oh...

Saul replied, "I saw my men scattering from me, and you didn't arrive when you said you would, and the Philistines are at Michmash ready for battle. So I said, 'The Philistines are ready...and I haven't even asked for the Lord's help!' So I felt compelled to offer the burnt offering myself before you came" (1 Sam. 13:11–12, with my emphasis).

I'm sure Saul was anticipating a "That's okay, buddy," maybe even a "You did what you had to. Good job leading your men!" Not the case! Samuel replied, "How foolish! You have not kept the command the Lord your God gave you." Ouch!

Even when we convince ourselves that we are solely focused on the Lord's will, we can actually be motivated by our own desires and perspective. And, friend, that is such a blurry line, I know. We want so badly to desire only the Lord, His will and His heart. We want to obediently follow Him because we love Him so stinkin' much. Unfortunately, the enemy uses our corrupted human nature to pollute these God-honoring desires with selfish motives. Then being the butthead that he is, Satan usually likes to trap us in one of two ways—either we blindly press forward, fooled into thinking we are chasing God's heart, or we remain frozen out of fear that we are actually being selfish and disobedient. He is the author of confusion and takes delight in paralyzing God's warriors.

How then can we determine when our roots are wrapped around God's heart or our own? We can start with our speech; Scripture tells us it is a direct overflow of our heart (Prov. 4:23).

Consider where Saul's heart was rooted when he responded to Samuel's reprimand: "I saw my men scattering from me, and you didn't arrive when you said you would, and the Philistines are at Michmash ready for battle. So I said, 'The Philistines are ready...and I haven't even asked for the Lord's help!' So I felt compelled to offer the burnt offering myself before you came" (1 Sam. 13:11–12, with my emphasis).

Count how many times Saul referred to himself or Samuel in those two verses. It's ten—ten stinkin' times. How many times did he refer to the Lord? Only once. Can you see how his speech gave his focus away? Can you see how his motives were truly rooted in himself, though he believed his actions were God-honoring?

Have our hearts compelled us to act when we should be still, convincing us that our points of view mirror the Lord's? Have we disguised our disobedient tongues in costumes of "faith" when He can plainly see them dressed to the nines in worry and doubt? Are our roots burying deep into His heart or withering in the shallow spirit of fear? Every single word we choose to utter will speak either life or death into our perspective. It's worth the effort to learn how to tame our tongues, my friend!

Just ask our buddy Saul. When the pressures of life threatened his peace, his resolve to take heart and wait buckled. His trust wavered. He reacted to the pressing and chose to take control. Sadly, when he took matters into his own hands and disobeyed God's command, he robbed himself of a magnitude of blessings the Lord had in store for him. Samuel told him, "Had you kept His command, the Lord would have established your kingdom over Israel forever. But now your kingdom must end" (1 Sam. 13:13–14).

Waiting is tough, especially when the enemy convinces us that we can help the Lord hurry our slow-moving train along. I'll remind you of this potent little secret, though—the Lord doesn't need our help. And let's be real, we don't really have a clue what we're doing or where we're going anyway, not really. It's one of the aspects of faith that makes it so wonderfully exhilarating (and slightly terrifying)! And, friend, I can say with confidence that as we wait, the Lord is preparing us for the incredibly beautiful gifts He has tailor-made for us. Just as Saul could not see the magnitude of blessings the Lord desired to lavish on him, neither can we see what joys are to come.

Let's learn from Saul's experience and resolve not to act in haste. There's a reason Satan desperately urges mankind into rushing time, as if time is actually ours to be had. The seasons of waiting, heartbreak, and longing are often where the Lord teaches us how to replace hurt with Him. He matches the intensity of your emotional despair with His overwhelming love and mercy. He shows you what an oasis your intimate moments with Him truly are. These seasons are where you learn the difference between the world's peace and His peace that surpasses all understanding (Phil. 4:7).

The idea of that happening gives the enemy hives. He'll do everything in his power to keep you from experiencing it. He will enslave you in your emotions and your longing for resolve. He'll use the idol of control to manipulate your human nature. Even better, he'll often cleverly try to disguise it all as a valiant, heavenly obedience. When we fall for his scheme, we hold the door open for him to stir up the chaos that he thrives on. We blindly walk into his trap of lies that if we just do a little more, we will finally see the change we think we want.

I know, I know, it is so natural to desire control. Everyone does struggle with it to some degree. But why do we accept it as an undeniable element of our lives? What would happen if we went against the "norm" and trained ourselves to resist the idol of control? What would it feel like to actually live with undaunted peace in the midst of life's mayhem?

I get it, though. We're still broken souls in a fallen world. We spend so much of our time wrestling with the king of chaos, who loves to terrorize our minds. Unfortunately, there is nothing we can do about the chaos itself, but we can suit up in the armor of God each and every day. If we commit to this spiritual training, will our hearts still occasionally ache and yearn in this life? Will we still wonder and fight the need to control? Absolutely. The unseen and unknown can be terrifying, especially with matters of the heart. To try to say otherwise is simply ignorant.

However, our freedom comes when, despite how we feel, we move in obedience anyway. It makes the Lord's daddy heart soar. The reality is that we'll never fully know what trials, blessings, lessons, and life await us, but we do know that God is already waiting for us in the middle of them all. Don't let that be cliché to you. Read it again. With a confident "Yes, Lord," you can boldly stride toward both the celebrations and the forest fires of this life, knowing He'll be firmly standing with you through them all.

CONNECT

What sentence, paragraph, or fact from this section could you relate to? Record it below.

When you read it, what was the first thought that crossed your mind? The first emotion you felt?

REFLECT

Can you think of a time when someone you know struggled with the Idol of Control? What did you notice about them and their situation, from the outside looking in?

Was there ever a season in your life where you felt the need to control the situation but now, you realize God saw things you didn't? What advice would you give your younger self about that season, if you could?

RESPOND

PRAISE. Name four specific praises for ways you can now see how God handled situations in your past, even if you couldn't see it then.

1.

2.

3.

4.

REPENT. Name three instances you have tried/are trying to control situations, emotions, or people, instead of trusting that God sees what you don't.

1.

2.

3.

ASK. Name two situations in which you are currently struggling to relinquish control in this season (think physically, emotionally, situationally, etc.).

1.

2.

YES, LORD. Name one realistic step you can take today to give the reins back to God regarding one of the above situations.

1.

CLING TO SCRIPTURE

And we know that in all things God works for the good of those who love him, who[a] have been called according to his purpose. (Romans 8:28)

Therefore do not worry about tomorrow, for tomorrow will worry about itself. Each day has enough trouble of its own. (Matthew 6:34)

Do not be anxious about anything, but in every situation, by prayer and petition, with thanksgiving, present your requests to God. (Philippians 4:6)

Which verse did you choose to commit to memory and utilize as you give back the reins? Record it below.

Battle V:
Your Inner Circle

WITNESS PROTECTION

We are all born with an instinct to observe and manipulate our surroundings, drawing conclusions about how the world works. This helps us to survive. Discoveries from past trial and error heavily influence our perspective of the world and its challenges. If you flip the switch on the wall, the monsters go away; if you drop the glass, it may shatter. If you leave cheesecake in the refrigerator overnight, it will magically disappear by morning—all valuable life lessons. We freely acknowledge these physical discoveries in life but ignore the emotional discoveries that mold and shape us into the humans we are, post-training wheels. For most, this instinct manifests in some destructive way at one time or another. For many, that manifestation alters their trajectory in life. For some, it cripples them until they can't recover.

Woah, that got deep. Did you feel it? We're going back to the whole fruit versus root concept. Let's back it on up and find some context, shall we? What if the way you express your emotions is rooted in an innate desire for approval and acceptance? WAIT! Don't close the book. Hear me out. I know that you're strong and confident and don't need the approval of others. High five, friend. (No, seriously, high five!) Keep reading, though.

No matter how strong, confident, bold, and fearless you are, the fact still remains that all humans are encouraged by praise from others. We may not need it to survive, but it definitely motivates us to know people are beside and behind us, cheering us on and believing in us.

The reality is that at some point, someone or something caused us to second-guess our choices. It may have been a verbal or nonverbal critique of something you said, did, didn't do, wore, laughed at, ate, believed, loved, disliked—the possibilities are endless. I'm sure I'm not the only one who can think of an instance for all of the categories above. When that happened, though, we didn't like the way it felt, and the natural tendency to observe and analyze the problem kicked in, probably without us realizing it. We adjusted and transformed aspects of ourselves to regain approval, then made a mental note to make sure it didn't happen again. Congrats, girl! You just added to your belief system of how the world works and what your role is in it. Remember middle school? High school? Yikes!

Let's talk about what happens when our foolproof system of figuring out life fails us. What happens when, no matter how you analyze and adjust, approval is not regained? Sure, shake off the stranger's opinion. Who cares? But what if it's someone you love? Someone who is supposed to love you? Someone you value and cherish? What then? Once the quest for validation begins, the process of losing ourselves commences.

Years down the road, we find ourselves living to gain others' approval, whether we realize it or not. Our past has taught us that finding validation in the eyes of others is finding confidence and purpose.

What makes you valuable? Is it your work? Is it a hobby? Is it your intelligence? Your appearance? What you own? Where you live? Who you dine with?

What do other people think of you? Your spouse? Your boss? Your friends? Your church family? Strangers?

How do you try to fill the void in your soul? Does it manifest in overworking? Overspending? Vanity? Moral compromises? Lies? Perfectionism? Overeating? Over exercising? Overthinking?

What suffocates you as a result? Anxiety? Anger? Depression? A critical spirit? Hopelessness? Isolation?

We so desperately seek to find our best selves in the eyes of others instead of Jesus. And by "we," I mean me—all me. I have battled the idol of approval my entire life. When I was young, I experienced the failure to gain approval from someone I loved dearly. I tried everything, changed everything I could think of, to be what I thought would make this person accept me, but it was never enough. I finally formed the conclusion that it wasn't something about me that was the problem. The problem was just me.

From that point forward, I believed every other person I came in contact with saw me as less than enough, so I was proactive in gaining their approval. I was a chameleon, y'all. My appearance, interests, and beliefs could change at the drop of a hat in order to be accepted by the friend-group of the week. I've been the tomboy, the girly girl, the prep, the country girl, and the skater (aka I just dressed like Avril's little sis). I've been the flirt, the secret-keeper, the bully, and the gossip. I've found my identity in being the wild child, someone's girlfriend, and the make-you-cringe, holier-than-thou Christian. I've found my value in my appearance and how well I did in school. I've been willing to be everything except myself because that girl had already missed the bar early on.

When nothing I tried received the approval I desired, I decided I didn't care what people thought of me. I didn't need others' approval or permission to be me. I was me, take it or leave it. (Please read that as the manipulative lie from the enemy that it was, instead of the confidence and self-love I believed it to be.)

Knowing now how I respond to words of affirmation, I see why I lost myself in a search for acceptance. As much as positive words and opinions hold the power to build me up and make my spirit soar, negative words and opinions absolutely shred my heart to pieces. It's taken years for me to stop taking to heart the opinions of people who aren't in my "circle." I wish I could say I'm naturally one of those people who can shake off negativity, but I'm not. Even though I usually choose not to engage with it, I have a tendency to mentally file away disapproval, keeping it as a reminder that I'm not as brave or bold as I think I am, that I'm setting myself up for rejection (again), that I can't actually be used by God.

Satan knows this, and he loves to throw my past choices and hurts in my face whenever a new opportunity presents itself. I'm sure he has done it to you too. There's a reason, girl! The enemy wants you to doubt yourself into isolation. He wants to paralyze your potential. He doesn't want you to experience freedom and see the beauty in your scars.

God designed us to thrive most when we are in community. He designed us to fiercely love and be loved because we are made in His image. He is radical, ridiculous, all-consuming, unapologetic love (1 John 4:8). That's why you feel the desire to pursue friendships and connect with others. Sure, everyone feels this desire differently, but we are designed to run this race together (Eccles. 4:12). God makes it clear that when two or more are gathered in His name, He is in the midst of them (Matt. 18:20). That's powerful.

If the enemy can use this God-given desire and the negative opinions of others to convince us that we aren't enough, he can keep us from connecting, healing, and thriving. If he can keep you suppressing your passion out of fear, he can keep whatever you're supposed to rock this world with from coming to fruition. He can dwindle your flame and rob you of the sanctifying journey Jesus wants to walk with you.

Here's a confession. This isn't some past struggle I have overcome and lived to tell about. Satan still attacks me with this lie. Though I recognize the schemes more easily now, he still tends to slither in and choke me with them when I least expect it. It usually resurfaces when I plant my feet and practice some form of godly obedience, such as writing this book. Y'all, my mind has been such a war zone lately that I found myself beginning to creep back into isolation.

When I realized I had once again fallen for the lie of not being enough, I was infuriated. I had already started writing this book. If you read the first section, "From One Warrior to

Another," you know how God flooded me with this task and lit my heart on fire for it. I was confident in the direction God was taking it because I knew that, without a doubt, this call was from Him. Less than twenty-four hours afterward, Satan started ambushing my mind, crippling my confidence. At that point, I had only told four people about the quest. I feared what others would say if I failed or, worse, if I succeeded.

A week later, I took a few days off from writing to enjoy a trip to the beach with Brock and some dear friends. During the trip, I decided to share my little secret with Meredith, who is one of my closest friends. She listened. She smiled. She was nothing but excited and supportive of me. I knew that she would keep it under lock and key. She would always be an encourager to me in this. It's just who she is.

An hour later, I panicked. I regretted telling her. Not because of her at all—no, it was my fear. What if I fail, and the book never gets published? Does she think this is ridiculous, even though she sounded supportive? Does she think that I have no business writing a book on waiting when others have waited longer? Who am I to write a book about waiting and obedience and Jesus? This is a joke. I'm a joke. What am I doing?

For the next few days, I thought through every horrific circumstance that could stem from me writing this book and sharing my heart. Will people think I am grasping at straws? Will they see me as a hypocrite because they know who I used to be? Will I be picked apart by people I don't even know? Will I lose relationships for reasons out of my control?

I wanted to tell my women's group at church so they could be praying over all of it, but—

What if they laugh?

What if they roll their eyes because other people have been waiting longer?

What if word gets out and it becomes gossip?

What if it fails? I'll be a joke.

I hope you noticed that none of these what-ifs were concerns for how my words would display Jesus to the world.

I wasn't questioning whether I was being obedient to Him. Every single fear was rooted in my need for the approval and acceptance of others. It was all rooted in fears of the flesh.

The question remained, do I let others in on the secret? Do I tell others who can pray over all of this? Do I keep it quiet and safe? This was a tricky question for my heart, especially after my experiences over the past seven months.

Before we started trying to get pregnant, I had made up my mind to be raw and real with those around me, to be honest with how God was working in my heart, mind, and life throughout the process. I resolved to be open about it all—the highs, the lows, and everything in between. This was new territory for me because I had always been the lone wolf in a crowd, never letting anyone in, not really. Over the past eight years, however, the Lord had slowly opened my eyes to see and experience the power of unmasked relationships. Through those pivotal moments, I have gained so much confidence. I've worked hard to lay down hesitation and doubt in order to allow my heart to be open and let others in. Like I've said, Satan does love an isolated soul, after all.

So I told the friends in my small group. I was open and honest about my thoughts and feelings. Everyone was so excited for us! It was encouraging (because approval). I was so thankful to have people by my side who celebrated my life with me. However, that flame was quickly extinguished when I shared my frustrations and fears with the group after a few months of negative tests.

"I mean, you haven't been trying that long, have you? There's no reason to feel frustrated yet," someone said.

As the words left her mouth, two other people tucked their head and smirked. Maybe it wasn't even about me. I don't know, but pairing the comment and reactions with Satan's screaming lie that no one actually cared, I crumbled internally (because disapproval). I felt the heat flood my face, and my heart knotted. Looking back, I wish I had just smiled and said (in a loving and grace-filled tone, of course), "I've learned that dreams and love aren't logical, friend. I know what statistics say on how long it can take. I know that others have waited far longer than this. I know I have plenty of time, but my heart yearns for the day I get to celebrate that gift with y'all. So yes, I am frustrated today, and that's okay." Instead, my approval instincts kicked in. I immediately agreed that feeling frustrated was silly, brushed it off, and internally resolved to never again mention this journey to anyone except to my closest friends. I truly think those words were meant as motivation, but they brought more discouragement than you could imagine.

I'm well aware it was my choice to take the comment that way. I could have made up my mind to ignore how it came off. Wouldn't that be wonderful if we could boss our heart around if logic and emotion suddenly decided to tag team and keep each other in check? It doesn't work that way, though. And quite frankly, I had no desire to set myself up to be stung by the words of others again. Even though she didn't offend me, those unintentional words hurt badly. How would intentionally rude and insensitive comments paralyze my soul then? I didn't plan to find out. I had tried open, raw, and real, but now it was time to close up shop in my mind and heart.

I sat confused, though. At this point in my life, I knew better than to isolate myself. I knew from experience what Satan could do with a secluded heart and mind. How would I share enough to keep from being alone while still guarding my heart? Look, I know that God's approval is all I need. I know that. I also know there are five million books written on that very statement. I probably own most of them, if we're being honest. I know the truth—what the Bible says. My question was not what God says about approval, isolation, or honesty. My question was, how would I protect my heart while honoring the Lord's call to community?

These are the moments when I am extra grateful for my sister-friends who pour wisdom into my life. These people are the ones I trust to speak the truth, hold me accountable, and love me fully. These women are my "discipleship band." If you take nothing else away from this book, I hope you have a new desire to find those who love you too much to watch you remain stagnant or grow stale.

Friend, the reality is that the more people you allow into these quiet places of your soul, the more chances there are for Satan to manipulate and wreak havoc in your heart and mind. The reality is that people, no matter how wonderful, are flawed—yes, even you. Sometimes, actions and words hurt, intentional or not. I'm sure my words have left deep scars in some people that I am not even aware of, and that breaks my heart to think about.

Something else to consider is that not everyone is going to have your best interest in mind. Sadly, there are many who allow the acts of comparison and competition to stir negative emotions in the pit of their soul. Their venomous emotions overflow into the lives of those around them. You can't control what others will say and do, and there will always, always be some form of opposition in this life. (Did you hear that, Jenna?) There will always be an emotional risk when you resolve to love others freely, which is beautiful and tragic, all at the same time.

The Lord gives us wisdom and discernment for a reason, y'all. My discipleship band helped me realize that I have to utilize those gifts when disclosing information to the world. They also reminded me that it is okay to have seasons of privacy. Privacy and isolation are not the same thing. When you are isolated, you are keeping everyone out, leaving yourself with nothing but your own perspective. When you are private, you have a select few friends that you are raw and open with—ones who speak truth to your situation and heart, who love you and battle with you full of joy, confidence, and peace.

I took a deep breath and accepted that our journey of starting a family would be a season of privacy in our life. We had a few people we would openly share our thoughts and emotions with—people who would love and lead us like Jesus. However, this season would not be a widely known adventure. Sometimes, when you are walking through obedience and practicing active faith, when your heart and mind don't play nicely, it is necessary to protect yourself. There is absolutely nothing wrong with that, and it doesn't mean God won't use your story for His glory.

But, friend, I can't wait for the day when you hold this book and read about my private season of pruning, of discovering a new level of who Jesus is. I can't wait to share all He teaches me about Himself, His love, and our relationship during this journey. I can't wait until the nagging lie that I am not talented enough, didn't wait long enough, or am not holy enough to write these truths is silenced. I can't wait to see how God will use all aspects of this adventure to bring glory to His name. I can't wait for the testimony that will come out of wading through the terrifying, humbling, exciting waters of waiting.

But for now, I will sip my coffee, listen to jazz music, and continue to record His story of our family in the quiet, knowing that at the perfect time, God will throw open the doors to our season of privacy. In the meantime, we will continue to link arms with our discipleship band as we find our "Yes, Lord" in this place of in-between.

DISCIPLESHIP FRIENDS

Maybe it's just me, but pulling weeds midday in Alabama's August heat often seems more appealing than developing new friendships. Much like dating, it can be exciting and exhausting all at the same time. There's always a mix of hesitation, skepticism, and eagerness as you learn more about the other person. Luckily, if things aren't going well, you quietly and gracefully disconnect from the person and move on with life.

As much of an introvert or loner as some people claim to be, the truth remains that we need friendships, y'all. I'm not referring to the surface-level, we-like-the-same-movies-and-Ben-and-Jerry's-flavor friendships, but the deep, know-your-darkest-corners-and-biggest-dreams kind. It's the kind of friendship where the other person can read your silence, anticipate your reactions, and show up at your door with cookie dough and a resolve to pull you out of the pit you've dug yourself into. The friendships where the other person is focused on your soul, excited for your future, and unwavering in their prayers for both. The friendships where excitement is rooted in making each other more like Jesus.

I know, I didn't know such friendships existed either. I had experienced estrogen bonds with other godly women before. Solidarity, sister! I have had the privilege of having friends who prayed for me, encouraged me, and celebrated with me throughout my entire life. In my adult life, I've even had women who genuinely loved me and the Lord, and I learned so much about Him through their example.

But y'all, I had never had friends who took my hand and dove headfirst into the crap in my heart, who forced me to look my past in the eye and deal with it, and who then helped me bury it at the foot of the cross and run full speed into Jesus's arms. I had never had friends who checked in about my soul, not just my life. I had never had friends who would consistently call my bluff because they knew I was better than the choices I was making. I had never had friends who wanted to lock arms and chase Jesus with me, knowing there was a good chance I'd trip and sling them to the ground with me. I had never had friends who would dive under me as I fell and push me back up and forward, toward the prize we had set our eyes on in the beginning.

Some of you reading this may have found your discipleship friends when you were young, even if you didn't realize that's what they were. Perhaps you've clung to them throughout life, and you're currently smiling as you read this, making a mental note to text them and remind them how much they mean to you. You so should! Put a reminder in your phone to do it more frequently.

I want to envy you. I wish so badly that I had those friendships when I was younger. A lot of heartache could have been spared, for sure! For me, I didn't start finding the women who would serve as my discipleship band until I was twenty-five.

Let me be clear here, in case my words have somehow become jumbled between the page and your mind. You can have genuine friendships, godly friendships, friendships worth far more than money can buy, and they be completely real, life-giving, and a total blessing to your life. However, it is possible to have a life full of these friendships and still not have your discipleship band. Your band is unique because the foundation of it is a dedication to intentionally and actively grow together, hold each other accountable in the journey, and strive to learn how to live like Jesus a little more each day.

I hope you didn't get stuck on the word *accountable* in the previous sentence. I roll my eyes when I hear that, as well, but I'm not referring to the buzz phrase "accountability partner," which is thrown so lackadaisically around in our Christian culture. You know what I'm talking about—the church camp challenge to "find a friend who will keep you accountable." No, true accountability goes so much deeper and is merely an attribute of a friendship rooted in disciple-making.

Discipleship friends dig through your dirt for you, judgment free, and pull you toward the cross. They help you target areas of weakness and support you in your growth. They know there will be seasons of trials and of triumphs, and they are excited to stand by your side through both. This type of friendship is truly a rarity in this life because we often have one or the other but not both. Sometimes, we have friends who know our dirt. They may have been there for us and with us during those seasons. They may offer encouragement and a safe place to pour your heart out. They may offer ways to distract us. They may even offer to pray for us. Unfortunately, many of these friends never reach down into the rough waters and pull you out in a way that leads you to Jesus. That, my friends, is hard. It's emotionally wrecking at times, and often they are met with resistance from your fearful, broken heart. It's a lot to ask, and most people just aren't willing to be your lifeboat and mirror all at the same time.

On the other hand, we may have friends who inspire us to lead godly lives, hold us accountable for showing up and finishing well, and teach us through their example. It's very possible that we inspire each other in some way! The pitfall comes when we realize that they don't know the dirt in our soul. I'm not talking just about past dirt and testimony, but about the here-and-now war for your soul. The isolation creeps in when we realize they don't know the quiet battles raging in our minds, nor do we really want them to. They don't know that we need rescuing because we have resolved to stay focused and dedicated, trusting that God will handle the rest. Meanwhile, we're drowning in ourselves.

Girl, you have to have both! God has handled it all. He has given us His Word, which teaches us about the necessity of Godly friends and discipleship. Both of these aspects—

knowing you intimately and pushing you toward the cross—are vital to your growth. Though He has given us direction on what to look for, we have to be brave enough to pursue it. But oh, friend, I'm speaking from experience when I tell you that when you do find and embrace these relationships, you will cling to them for dear life. They will be refreshing to your heart and soul. They will give you confidence you didn't realize you were lacking. They will help make a disciple of you as you go out to proclaim His name in your Jerusalem, wherever that may be, and to the ends of the earth (Acts 1:8).

Obviously, discipleship friends are extremely important. Knowing this, I struggled with narrowing down biblical characters to write about, in order to display the gift these friendships have to offer. I had three examples in mind, and I couldn't decide. Then one day I thought, "Hey, genius! This is your book. You can write about all of them!" So that's what I chose to do. Each of these friendships has opened my eyes to what a disciple-based friendship truly looks like. I hope they inspire your heart as well.

Moses and Aaron

I love these dudes. You know who Moses is—the baby in a basket floating down the river, later declaring "Let my people go!" We're going to skip the beginning and fast-forward a bit until we get to the part where Moses sees the burning bush. If you're not familiar with the story, Moses was going about his business, tending his father-in-law's flock, when he wandered to Mount Sinai. There he was drawn to a bush that was engulfed in flames yet not burning up. As Moses inched closer to investigate, God started speaking to him from within the bush. During that conversation, God told Moses that He had heard the cries of the people of Israel, who were currently enslaved by Pharaoh. He was sending Moses to confront Pharaoh and lead the Israelites out of Egypt.

Caught up? Okay, so we know Moses has just been told he is being sent to rescue God's chosen people. What does he do? Puff out his chest and shout a battle cry? Nope, he protests. He questions. He panics. "Who am I to appear before Pharaoh? Who am I to lead the people of Israel out of Egypt?" (Exod. 3:11). God, being the good Father that He is, reassured Moses that he wouldn't have to face any of it without Him (3:12).

Pause. Don't let it be lost to you that Moses is actually conversing with God in this moment—not praying to Him but actually conversing. The Lord has audibly explained the task at hand and has reassured Moses that He will be with him through it all. I know I just said that, but let it really sink in. The warm fuzzy I feel when I hear my loved ones utter words of support makes my heart soar. I can't imagine how my heart would feel hearing God speak those words aloud to me!

Still, despite hearing the voice of God, Moses continues to protest, this time with a different concern. Actually, he protests three times, each time presenting God with a different what-if scenario. When the Lord gives him explanations and answers for all of his concerns, Moses runs out of ideas and begins pleading that God would send someone else instead. "O Lord, I'm not very good with words. I never have been, and I'm not now, even though you have spoken to me. I get tongue-tied, and my words get tangled...Lord, please! Send anyone else" (Exod. 4:10, 13).

What a big ole baby! The Lord has called Moses and promised to be with him and provide everything he will need to succeed. Even still, we see him cowering, begging for someone else to take his place. What. A. Weenie.

If God ever rolls His eyes at us, I can picture Him doing it in this moment. Even though Moses had made Him angry (4:14), the Lord offered yet another solution to his panicked pleas. "What about your brother, Aaron the Levite? I know he speaks well...Talk to him, and put the words in his mouth. Aaron will be your spokesman to the people" (Exod. 4:14–16).

All right, let's dissect this a bit. The first aspect of disciple friendships that we see from this story is this: the Lord always provides a way for us to grow when we ask. Sometimes it's strategies. Sometimes it's answers. Sometimes it's other people. Sometimes it's opportunities for practice. In this instance, He gave Moses someone who was strong where he was weak, someone whom Moses could lean on and depend on, someone that would stand beside him and help him fulfill the call God placed on his life, even when he felt intimidated and insecure.

When I think of my discipleship band, this theme rings true. I think about Aly's gentleness. I think about her ability to make time stand still and bring my frantic mind back to focus. I think about Laura's passion and hunger for God. I think about her eagerness to shout YES to His call and her dedication to see those she loves bloom into all God has created them to be. I think of Kaylee's contagious, undaunted joy and Jesus-goggles she views her world through. That's good stuff and all areas I need to become stronger in. Actually, these are areas I have begged the Lord for YEARS to grow me in. I love that He gave me discipleship sisters to lead by example as I learn exactly what that looks like.

Back to the story. Now that Moses has Aaron by his side, we see them embark on the quest laid before them. Side by side, they called the elders together to speak with them. Aaron spoke and Moses performed the miraculous signs, just as the Lord had instructed (Exod. 4:30). They were the dynamic duo, I tell ya! When they finished speaking with the Israelite elders, the Word tells us the two went and spoke to Pharaoh. When Pharaoh wouldn't listen, the team amped it up a bit. They persisted and declared their request once again to the ruler (Exod. 5:2–3). I love that change in the verbs used! Just visualize it. They went from merely speaking to Pharaoh about their requests to *persisting* and *declaring* them. That's one of the beauties of having your discipleship friends by your side— when you complement each other's weaknesses and make a powerful team, you gain confidence and boldness in your calling that you may not have had otherwise.

Throughout the next few chapters of Exodus, we see God instructing Moses and Aaron together, with Aaron speaking and Moses performing signs with the anointed shepherd's staff. However, we start to see a shift in chapter 8. This time when Moses and Aaron address Pharaoh to warn of the coming plague, we see Moses speak and Aaron perform the sign with the staff. Don't breeze past this tiny shifting of gears in the story! It is such an awesome display of how these friendships can and should work in our lives.

Neither of these men were wise old sages by any means. Aaron had never done anything like this before, but He trusted Moses's word about the call on their lives. He trusted that Moses would not lead them astray, even if it did sound absurd at times. Moses had never done anything like this before, either. Over time, as they continued to work together and act in obedience, Aaron's example taught Moses how to speak with confidence. In turn, Moses's example taught Aaron how to be a mighty vessel for the Lord. Now we see them bravely switch roles. The Lord equipped one through the influence of the other. Both men were radically changed as a result. When you're part of a discipleship band, you not only offer each other encouragement, but you also challenge and help each other grow in areas of weakness.

By the time the Israelites cross the Red Sea and walk in deliverance, we see Moses both speaking and performing the signs himself (Exod. 14:15–31). When I was reading through this story and realized what had happened from beginning to end, I sat back in awe. Crybaby Moses had transformed into a bold, confident leader. The Lord equipped him by giving him a friend that would teach and strengthen him through his example. Aaron stood by Moses through both the trials and triumphs. Slowly, Moses grew in his confidence until he took his place and led the Israelites out of Egypt, fulfilling the original call on his life. It's incredible to think about. It encourages me to be an Aaron to my friends, just as they so often are for me.

The lesson doesn't end there, though. It makes me smile that as you keep reading, you see Moses and Aaron still working side by side for the Lord. Moses had found his confidence in leadership, yes, but more importantly, he had found his faithful friend who supported him in that role of leader (Exod. 16). We never read of Aaron becoming jealous or resentful when Moses began confidently speaking and acting on his own. Envy never got the best of him as he watched his friend lead the Israelites into freedom. No, Aaron understood that it was a God-ordained call on his friend's life, and he was content doing whatever was needed to support his brother and friend.

One of my favorite Moses-and-Aaron stories displays this rare support system so beautifully. In the story, the Israelites were attacked by the warriors of Amalek. Moses commanded one of his warriors to take some men and physically fight back while he went to the top of the nearby hill and held up the anointed staff to call the power of God down (Exod. 17:8–9). This was a brilliant idea. We read next that "as long as Moses held up the staff in his hand, the Israelites had the advantage. But whenever he dropped his hand, the Amalekites gained the advantage" (Exod. 17:11).

I want you to take a moment and imagine holding a tree limb above your head all day. If you've done any form of an arm workout or even just raised your hands in praise on a Sunday morning, you can imagine how exhausting this all-day feat would be. Think of how fatigued your arm would feel after only a few minutes. Now imagine knowing that if you dropped your arm, you would be risking your family's lives. Can you imagine the pressure he felt in his arms, mind, and heart? I wouldn't be surprised if he had tears streaming down his face in pure resolve and pain.

Luckily, Aaron was there. He and another man named Hur set a marvelous example of how discipleship friends support each other when facing insurmountable pressures in this life. Moses' arms soon became so tired he could no longer hold them up. So Aaron and Hur found a stone for him to sit on. Then they stood on each side of Moses, holding up his hands (Exod. 17:12).

Did they comfort him by saying, "Oh, friend, my heart breaks for you! I'm praying for you"? Did they say, "I can't imagine what you feel like! I'm here to talk if you need me"? Did they try to encourage him by saying, "Be strong. This is the Lord's will. Fight through it. You can do it"? No, they didn't—none of that. Did you read that they tried to figure out how Moses could let his arms down and rest? Did you read where they tried to take the staff from him to relieve the pain? Nope, ya didn't.

As wonderful as words of encouragement and willingness to lend a helping hand are, that is not always what is needed. These friends knew good and well that Moses's battle went much deeper than those temporary fixes. They knew that he had to fulfill what the Lord was calling him to do. They knew he had to keep his hands raised and no one could do it for him. They also knew their friend was in excruciating pain, which was going to be part of his call in that battle. The Bible doesn't say they even uttered a word to Moses during this time. They didn't try to change what God was doing. What they did was assess the situation and take action to support him in the moment.

They offered the only relief they had access to that wouldn't interfere with his mission. They rolled a rock over for him to sit on to alleviate pressure and pain in his back. Then they came beside him and held his hands up. They didn't hold the staff for him. That was Moses's job. They simply came beside their friend and held his hands up when life threatened to weigh him down.

The whole story is so inspiring, y'all. Discipleship friends don't try to minimize what God is doing in your life. They don't try to magically fix everything. They trust that the Lord knows what He is doing. They pray for you, and they lean into the Holy Spirit's leading to know what their role is. They rally around you in support, so you don't have to weather the storms alone.

Elizabeth and Mary

"Thanks for being my Elizabeth."

Laura sent this text to me one morning. I wish I could say I immediately smiled and sent one right back, thanking her for being my Elizabeth too. Unfortunately, I didn't have a clue what she was talking about. I knew Elizabeth was John's mother. I knew that she was Mary's cousin. I knew that John leapt in Elizabeth's womb when he heard pregnant Mary's voice. Aside from that, I had nothing. After listening to sermons and reading more about Mary and Elizabeth in Luke 1, my heart soared.

When we find Elizabeth and Mary in the Gospel of Luke, Mary has just been visited by an angel who tells her she will be giving birth to the Messiah. Remember all those emotions we pictured her having when we discussed her? The flour dust had settled, and there was middle-school Mary, left to take in the reality of what she had just been told.

The first thing she does is run to Elizabeth. It doesn't say, but I can guess she may have felt pretty fearful. At this point, she'd probably started going through all of the ramifications of being pregnant and giving birth to the Savior—potentially losing Joseph and her family, being labeled as an adulteress, the whole pressure of raising-the-Messiah thing. I can totally see her bursting through the door, on the verge of tears, with a frantic look in her eyes. Can you picture it? Sweet girl! But do you know what Elizabeth does in response?

"Elizabeth gave a glad cry and exclaimed to Mary, 'God has blessed you above all women, and your child is blessed'" (Luke 1:42). I can only imagine what those simple statements did for Mary's heart. I can imagine it is much of what Aly,

Laura, and Kaylee's words do to mine. Here she was, probably physically tired and hungry from traveling during her first
trimester. More than likely, she was emotionally spent, having
been left to her own thoughts about everything during her
journey. There's no telling what was going through her head
when she arrived! But her friend met her with unrestrained joy
and celebration. She was quick to remind Mary that she was
blessed, despite what else she may be thinking or feeling in
the moment and despite what anyone else may try to convince her of. This reaction encouraged Mary's spirit so much
so that it inspired her famous song of praise.

I love the Elizabeths in my life. When Satan tries to distract my heart with chaos and warped perspective, my discipleship sisters remind me that I am blessed. They help me
recognize the joy that the enemy is trying to steal from me.
They celebrate the everyday victories in my life. They encourage my spirit and spark the song in my soul.

Naomi and Ruth

The last friendship I want to highlight is one that proves
what the enemy intends for evil, the Lord will always use for
our good (Gen. 50:20). Meet Naomi and Ruth. Technically,
Naomi is Ruth's mother-in-law, but as their story unfolds,
we see the sweet relationship that has formed between the
two of them.

Naomi had a husband and two sons. Both sons married,
one to a woman named Orpah and the other to a woman
named Ruth. We learn in Ruth 1:5 that both of Naomi's sons
and her husband passed away, leaving her with her two
daughters-in-law. Left with the nearly impossible task of making ends meet, Naomi, Orpah, and Ruth headed toward the
land of Judah because word had spread that crops were boun-
tiful there. On the way, Naomi advised the women to return
to their mothers' homes. She wished them well, hoping they

would find new marriages and success in life. When she said this, they all broke down and wept (Ruth 1:6–9).

That last sentence alone gives such insight to the depth of love they felt for each other. It was painful for them to go their separate ways. Both women insisted that they continue on with Naomi, but their mother-in-law replied, "Why should you go on with me?...No, my daughters, return to your parents' homes, for I am too old to marry again...Things are far more bitter for me than for you, because the Lord Himself has raised his fist against me" (Ruth 1:11–13).

Naomi loved "her daughters" so incredibly much. She was trying to look out for their well-being by sending them back to a home where she knew they would have a blessed future ahead of them. She didn't want them to have to stick around and endure what she anticipated was in store for her. There would probably be a lot of sorrow. There may be social conflict, considering she was now widowed and alone, too old to remarry. There would probably be many hardships, as far as her quality of living was concerned. She knew all this, so she selflessly urged them to leave her and go about their own lives, even though it was probably tearing her own heart to shreds.

Orpah took Naomi's advice, wept once more, and kissed her goodbye (Ruth 1:14). Ruth, on the other hand, didn't budge. When Naomi realized Ruth wasn't following Orpah's lead and turning back, she tried to persuade her once more to return to her family. The way Ruth replies to her makes my soul smile, "Don't ask me to leave you and turn back. Wherever you go, I will go; wherever you live, I will live. Your people will be my people, and your God will be my God" (Ruth 1:16).

Now look, I realize we women won't literally follow our friends around in this life. I realize that sometimes circumstances and distance pull us away from relationships we love and cherish. Hello! It's the story of most of my adult life. I ask you to peer deeper into her words, though. Let's break them down and look at them more closely.

"Don't ask me to leave you and turn back." This makes me tilt my head in awe to think of just how much mutual adoration and respect is between them. I love that Naomi was trying to be selfless, anticipating the hard times Ruth would face if she stayed. When I visualize Naomi stopping mid journey to force a smile and encourage the women to turn back, even though it meant she would truly be alone, my heart aches for her. To think of the mixed emotions she must have felt kissing Orpah goodbye and watching her walk away brings tears to my eyes.

But to think of how even when Naomi tried to push her to go, Ruth dug her heels in and clung to the woman, unwavering in her loyalty, makes those tears fall freely. Discipleship friends are in it for the long haul. They don't fade in rough seasons. They are the ones who stand by you and hold your hands up when they are weak, remember? They are the ones who are willing to weather the storms with you because you are worth every minute of it in their eyes.

"Wherever you go, I will go; wherever you live, I will live." Again, it was literal for Ruth and Naomi, yes, but that isn't usually the case for the rest of us. We can gain such insight into biblical friendship when we read this, though. When I digest these words, I think of my beautiful Aly. The Lord brought us together when my husband and I were living in Jasper. By the time the Lord called us to move again, Aly and I were seeing each other three to five times a week, pursuing the Lord and our goals together, and feeling completely in awe of God's gift of our friendship. By moving, it would increase our travel time to each other's front door from five minutes to two hours.

I'll admit it. I was nervous that our friendship would fade with distance and the demands of everyday life, but it hasn't. We may not be physically together day in and day out like we used to be, but we are still so involved in each other's lives. We have both stood by each other in seasons of refining fire since the move, and it is such a testament to our friendship. Without hesitation, we can confidently say we are in it for the long haul. (Wakeboarding with the grandbabies, right, Aly?) Her love goes where I go. We are still a safe place for each other to land. Her heart lives where mine does. If I am celebrating, so is she. If I am hurting, so is she. If I am striving, she is praying. If I am defeated, she lifts my hands. After spending time with her, whether in person or through the gift of technology, my heart is closer to Jesus, and that is extraordinarily beautiful.

"Your people will be my people." When moving frequently left Brock and I feeling like the new kids, it made our hearts soar to find people who embraced us with open arms. Unwilling to let us hang out on the sidelines, they joyfully drew us into their world. They opened their homes and their hearts, and God used their love to draw us closer to Him. Over time, they became family ("framily," if you will). We absolutely, positively adore them, their children, and their extended families. They are now "our people," and we are theirs. They walk beside us during all seasons of life, including this season of privacy. Just as we go to battle in prayer for them, they are storming the gates for us as well. Knowing there are people who choose, love, and pray over you unprompted will motivate and empower you in the mountains and the valleys of this life.

"And your God will be my God." This is the most important piece of this puzzle, y'all. Out of everything we've discussed, this is how you will know that you have found your discipleship band—without hesitation, you will lock arms and fall headfirst into Jesus together.

I have many friends who love Jesus and desperately seek His heart and will. They will pray for me. They will support me. They will read books and devotionals with me. They encourage my growth. However, they are not my discipleship band, nor am I theirs. That doesn't make our friendship any less special or authentic, but it is necessary to clarify the difference between the two.

I only have a few friends that make my soul a priority. We're talking two or three people here. The relationship we have is just different. We are constantly turning each other's eyes toward Jesus as He molds us into the kingdom warriors we're called to be. We willingly trudge through the swamps and joyfully soar through the clouds together. We run to each other when we're broken and under attack. It never crosses our mind to withhold any part of our journey from each other. We aren't afraid of becoming a burden or being judged. We care far too much to allow one another to make camp in any kind of comfort zone. We boldly belt each other's redemption song when this world tries to wear us down. We run to each other to celebrate, to cry, to dream, and to live.

Have you found the friends who offer godly strength to combat your weaknesses? Have you found friends who can teach you to be more like Jesus? Who can help you grow in your calling from Him? Have you found the friends who respect your journey and come by your side to support you in it, whatever that looks like from moment to moment? The friends who hold your hands up when life weighs down your soul? Have you found the people who will sing to your heart when Satan whispers his age-old lies? Have you found the friends who are quick to silence the chaos in your mind and refocus your eyes to see the blessing in front of you? Have you found the friends who are with you for the long haul, who won't waver with the changes of life, who will love your family as their own? Have you found the friends who not only love Jesus but make it their mission to walk with, carry, and some-times drag you down your path of sanctification in Him? Have you found your discipleship band?

Find your Ruth. Find your Elizabeth. Find your Aaron.

Find the ones who will share your cry of "Yes, Lord" as they stand firmly by your side through it all.

CONNECT

What sentence, paragraph, or fact from this section stuck with you most? Record it below.

What did it make you think and feel? Be specific.

REFLECT

Have you ever experienced a situation in a past friendship that caused you to be hesitant in pursuing future friendships? What unfounded "truth" did that situation cause you to adopt about yourself, life, or other people? How does it impact your choices now?

Have you ever witnessed a discipleship friendship (not your own)? What do you remember most about that particular pair of friends?

RESPOND

PRAISE. Name four people in your life who inspire you to pursue Jesus, even if they aren't your close friends or discipleship band.

1.

2.

3.

4.

REPENT. Name three times in the past your words or actions could have caused others to think less of themselves, (even if they "started it"!).

1.

2.

3.

ASK. Name two situations that you need The Lord to heal you from in regard to what you have to offer in friendship and/or this world.

1.

2.

YES, LORD. Name one step you can take toward establishing your discipleship band. (Is it making sure conversations are God-honoring? Actions? Is it finding someone you can be honest with about your struggles to hold your arms up? (If so, who?)

1.

CLING TO SCRIPTURE

Do not be misled: "Bad company corrupts good character." (1 Corinthians 15:33)

One who has unreliable friends soon comes to ruin, but there is a friend who sticks closer than a brother. (Proverbs 18:24)

Walk with the wise and become wise, for a companion of fools suffers harm. (Proverbs 13:20)

Which verse did you find or choose that you will commit to memory and utilize as you seek to establish discipleship based friendships? Record it below.

Battle VI:
Recognizing
The Enemy
And Regaining
Lost Ground

THE DEVIL IN DISGUISE

"How does Satan try to trip you up?"

Many of the answers were as expected—jealousy, temptation, frustrating people at work, unpredictable schedules, sickness. Sometimes the enemy's schemes are so obvious and anticipated that we can visualize him hiding in plain sight with a tripwire, giggling as if we can't see what he's up to.

"How do you ALLOW Satan to trip you up?"

Silence. This was a thinker—not because anyone was holier than thou, but because modern-day Christianity has trained our brains to see ourselves as helpless victims being pegged with Satan's spiritual dodgeballs. Eventually, answers started emerging.

"I do things I shouldn't. I snap at people instead of holding my tongue. I think about stuff that I shouldn't. I gossip...I mean vent about people that irritate me. I don't say anything when I know something isn't right. I judge people, even if I don't say anything about it. I doubt God." We could have gone on for hours if we had kept thinking on the topic.

Before you roll your eyes and think it was a holy-guilt trip issued upon us, it wasn't. Remember the spiritual dodgeballs? Human nature casts blame much faster than it accepts responsibility. I think about my first graders who are quick to tell me something ugly a friend said to them yet conveniently leave out the fact that it was a retaliation comment. How often do we shake our finger at Satan and his schemes while sidestepping our role in the madness?

When my husband walked into my life, I was recovering from a season of annihilated trust from multiple people, including myself. I had lost who I was while trying to find my footing, and I was a numb, shell of a woman with a beaming smile and a hesitant heart. Some of the people I had trusted most left me broken. The extent of the external and internal chaos in my life left me running on fumes.

We met by chance through a mutual friend we were both visiting. From that first day, Brock was so *different*. He carried himself with a steady peace, feeling no need to prove himself to those around him. As we started dating and learning more about each other, he had a constant, quiet assurance to him. He became a safe place in the midst of my storms. He met each of my skeletons with grace, love, and truth. He had no expectations of me, and I felt like I was free to breathe and truly be myself.

We have always brought out the very best in each other. It's not uncommon for people who are just meeting us to smile and say something along the lines of "Being around you two is so refreshing" or "Y'all give the rest of us hope." As encouraging as it is, we are both well aware that the difference everyone sees and feels is none other than the Holy Spirit. From early on, we decided to give our relationship to the Lord. I had tried dating the secular way, and it left me drained, frustrated, and worn. As much as I hated to admit it, I didn't know what God-honoring dating even looked like. (It's way more than abstaining, by the way.) Brock met the challenge with patience and joy and stepped into His role as spiritual leader far sooner than he was required to. He led (and still leads) us well, and I love him for that.

I had many moments during our two years of dating that I felt unworthy of Brock. I would look at this wonderful man, full of strength, peace, and joy, who saved himself for his bride and continually held himself to a higher standard than this world. I would compare what we had to offer each other and weep. In the world's standards, I had a lot going for me, but the most important parts of my soul were as wrecked and broken as you could imagine.

Knowing what I know now, that was all Satan. Christ convicts and empowers you with hope. Condemnation and shame are not from the Lord, but no one had ever taught me the difference between the two, much less pointed out who the voice inside my head really was. I remember the day I finally broke and let Brock in on the battle in my mind. He looked at me, smiled, and said, "If Jesus has already forgotten all of those things, who am I to hold them against you? Jenna, you are nothing I ever pictured for myself and everything I didn't realize I needed. Those thoughts you're having are not from Jesus."

I know. It sounds like a line from a cheesy romance movie, but those few sentences did more for my heart, my healing, and my confidence than he will ever realize. Eight years later, Brock is still the one that I can't wait to talk to at the end of my day, trust unfailingly to stand by my side as we brave the mountains and valleys of life together, and want to lay on our bedroom floor with, daydreaming about our future. At the time of this writing, we only have six years of marriage under our belt so far, but we already have such a rich testimony of how God can heal wounds, restore hope, and bless a life together when it's submitted to Him. It's absolutely incredible. There are days that I still can't believe it's our story.

It's not surprising that Satan desperately wants to corrupt that gift of ours. Brock and I learned early on just how much Satan HATES marriage. Considering it was created to be a tangible representation of God's love for His church (Eph. 5:22–32), there is something so potent about the thriving marriage of two Jesus-lovin' people in a world that has deemed the whole notion of it ridiculous. There is something special about a marriage that is ordained, blessed, and fiercely protected by the Lord. There is something so powerful about the two battling together in prayer for each other and the kingdom as a whole, "Where two or more are gathered" (Matt. 18:20). When a Jesus-lovin' married couple prays together, it leaves Satan shaking in his boots. You can see why he HATES marriage.

Knowing this though, we can all anticipate attacks—because they're coming, y'all! Unfortunately, it's part of this life. The enemy doesn't care how much you love Jesus and pray over your marriage and home. He is still going to try to throw curveballs your way. He's like a gnat. That's exactly why newlyweds are warned to be proactive and protective of their marriage. We are warned to be vigilant and to recognize times and ways we are vulnerable both as individuals and a couple. We are taught to pray over specific areas for each other and communicate openly about what is going on in our hearts and minds. We are taught to practice forgiveness, as hard as it may be sometimes. As long as we are in our biblical roles, we are taught to truly grasp that we are two broken people committed to walking hand in hand, helping each other grow.[3]

Brock and I have had our valleys. We've both been on the side of offender and forgiver—such is life! Having committed to practice open communication and present everything to each other—good, bad, and ugly—we have been able to avoid being blindsided with attacks, for the most part. Not that they don't still come; we just recognize them for what they are, and we refuse to let them divide us. Honestly, once you're well-practiced in keeping an eye out, many of Satan's schemes are painfully predictable. However, we can't discount that he is also smart and crafty at times. I've already experienced this personally, and hear me when I say he will try to silently sneak in when life leaves you distracted, even if the distractions are good.

---

[3] I want to note here that if the marriage is functioning how God designed it to, there should be no danger to either spouse, in any way. If you find yourself in a dangerous situation, even if your spouse claims the name of Jesus, something is not right. Scripture is clear that God is love. If it's not love, it's not God. Please see our resources in the back of this book if you find yourself needing help.

Routine. I love it. It loves me. We go together like peanut butter and jelly. When Brock and I were first married, I was absolutely ecstatic about getting to establish our environment together. Being able to create our own small retreat on this earth that accommodated our specific quirks and routines brought so much joy to my heart. It was mine. He was mine. This life I was living was actually mine. Can you believe it? I couldn't. Those first few years together were the most humbling, empowering, sweetest days, as we learned on a new level what life with each other, pursuing and uplifting, truly entailed. It set the tone for our marriage, and I would never trade that time for anything.

Over the handful of years we've had so far, our love has continued to grow deeper. We've grown individually and together—our likes and dislikes, dreams and motivations, our walk with Christ and His calling on our lives and marriage. We've found our groove and settled in, and I can honestly say the season of our marriage that we are currently in, even with the waiting and pruning, is the sweetest one yet. You can imagine my heartbreak, panic, and anger when I realized that the enemy was trying to use this blessing of stability to silently slink himself into our home and our marriage. Worse, my actions were allowing Him to do so.

Nothing dramatic happened. There was no major argument or moment full of heartbroken tears from confession. No, this was way more discreet than any of the obvious ways he tries to weasel himself in. Honestly, I didn't realize anything was in danger until I started practicing active surrender in this waiting game. As they say, hindsight is 20/20. I can see how Satan started manipulating the situation without us feeling any impact or inkling of his presence. Since I had taken my eyes off of the cross and allowed my heart and mind to be distracted by life, I was only aware of his obvious grenades tossed our way. As I continued to focus more and more on trying to grow our family, my guard was lowered, and the door cracked just enough for him to start wiggling himself into the picture.

From the outside looking in, everything seemed fine. Honestly, from the inside looking in, everything seemed fine. We were still respecting each other. We were still going out of our way to spend time together and serve each other. We were keeping our date nights blocked off as sacred time. We were still fulfilling one another's needs. We were very content and happy with where we were. The root of the problem wasn't in any actions. It was wholly my mind and heart. I can now see where it was starting to manifest and influence my actions, though no one would have ever known it.

Even though my actions said otherwise, my priorities were all out of whack! As I've already shared, my heart's focus wasn't fully on Jesus during the beginning of this journey. Sure, I started out with the best intentions to cruise through this adventure in the passenger seat, but I quickly tried to take control of the details surrounding the trip. I had surrendered to Him with selfish motives. I had been obsessing on how I could control the outcome. I stopped seeking Him and started seeking answers. My relationship with the Lord was blurred by all of my ridiculousness, and Brock and I fall under Him in hierarchy. So it goes without saying that my focus on Brock would be blurred as well. I can look back now and see how my focus was half-hearted when it came to our marriage. Though it wasn't intentional, our trying to get pregnant was constantly in the forefront of my mind, seeping into every single aspect of our life together.

Over the years, we've made it a habit to sit down and enjoy dinner together every night. We have some of our most meaningful conversations during this time, sometimes talking far longer than it takes to finish our dinner. I love it. This is one way Brock actively pursues me. He's not much of a talker, but he knows it makes me feel cherished when he takes time to sincerely talk and listen to what I have to say. He also helps me clean up after dinner. He turns on music, and we sing and dance around the kitchen. It doesn't matter what my day looks like; this always fills me to the brim with joy. You know you have a keeper when he makes you look forward to cleaning the kitchen after a long day!

I felt horrible when I realized I had stopped appreciating this gift. I felt worse when I realized I was only giving him a small portion of my focus during this time, even though he was still doing all he could to focus on me and love me well. Though I would listen and respond, I would also be thinking of data that needed to be logged. I would be calculating how many days we had until the fertile window and what our schedule looked like around that time. I would be thinking about different things I wanted to research to see if it would help our chances. Even when I would catch myself and try to refocus with sincerity, I would find my mind drifting back to all things fertility related. Sadly, this was only one area of our time together that was polluted by my need to control our journey to pregnancy.

As it was happening, it didn't seem like anything was off. We were still talking at dinner, cleaning and dancing around the kitchen, and enjoying time together before bed. We were still laughing and sharing and being completely in love. In my mind, all the research and tracking was just part of it. We've never braved this new terrain, after all. We knew NOTHING! After God opened my eyes to truly give this journey back to Him and take control of my compulsions, I was able to see how Satan had already started to steal this precious gift from us.

It was a heart matter. I had allowed these special moments of our day to turn into a routine. Though I still walked through our days and these times with my husband, I had stopped taking delight in him and our marriage. I vividly remember the day God convicted me of letting our marriage turn into just another thing we had, another detail of life in my mind. As Brock talked about his day at dinner that night, I soaked in every word and detail. I admired the cheesy, small aspects of him—how his eyes dance when he tells a funny story, how he throws his head back and laughs so loudly it echoes through the house, how his eyes seem to pierce my soul when I'm talking to him about something serious. Y'all, I didn't realize how I had lost my infatuation with Brock until I felt it again, until I put my whole heart back into our moments together and felt the butterflies that he's never failed to give me.

He had not changed at all. Our lives had not changed. If anything, they had become more stable. I, however, had tamed the intimacy between us because I wasn't fully present. When I say intimacy, please realize I'm not just referring to bedroom intimacy. Intimacy is so much more than what happens behind closed doors. It's the intense emotion you feel during a conversation. It's the belly laugh and bear hugs as you dance around the kitchen, making more mess than you are cleaning. It's holding hands in the car without talking. It's taking in the moment and realizing how lucky you are to have each other. It's marriage. Why in the world do we let ourselves forget the simple, blissful magic that it brings to our lives? I think about all of the spouses that lose their better half far too soon in this life, and it breaks my heart to think of the minutes we waste by allowing our marriage to become part of the mundane. As a whole, we have to do better, y'all.

I hope you hear the passion and love behind my words. I hope the enemy hasn't found a way to twist them in your heart to think I'm preaching or that I have some kind of fairy tale that others, maybe even you, can't relate to. I hope, if you've tuned me out and rolled your eyes—only still reading this because you hate not finishing chapters of a book—you will go back and reread the last page. I pray you will feel motivation to take back any ground the enemy has stealthily stolen from you and corrupted over the years.

We all go through seasons of distractions. Some distractions are obvious, like a stressful workplace, health issues, or financial burdens. Some are even an amazing blessing, like little feet running around, finishing your degree, or embarking on a new adventure that takes you out of your comfort zone. I just want to encourage you to stay vigilant during those times, girl. Don't let Satan use your heart and dedication to take your eyes off Jesus. Don't let your focus on your relationship with

Him become blurred by aspects of this life, even those that are blessings from Him.

I'm speaking from a place of humility and painful experience when I urge you to check in with yourself often because the Butthead is great at manipulating and deceiving. It's terrifying to realize how sly he can be in taking over, how easily stuff has the potential to unravel if you are not hypervigilant to the treasures of your life.

It has motivated me to truly check my heart, referring to both my priorities and the intentions behind them. It's motivated me to pray fiercely over my family and friends, which includes praising God simply for the gift they are. It's made me intentional about soaking up every moment I'm given with them. It's made me excited to take delight in the blessings of these days because they are the most valuable parts of my life.

God took what was meant to come between us, healed it, and made the fire blaze again, like He's always promised He would (Gen. 50:20). All I had to do was refocus on the cross, and He handled the rest, like He always does. This lesson alone is worth the season of waiting. Having fresh fire, focus, and adoration for the magnitude of blessings He's already freely given me makes my giddy heart race, dance around my kitchen, and sing, "Yes, Lord!"

EVE

Every time I read Eve's story, I would picture her as an airheaded woman who really doesn't know what she wants—she has no backbone, everything sounds good to her, and she sways whichever way the wind blows. Basically, I've always seen her as a ditz. Oh, nay nay! The Lord has helped me see her in a whole new light. Just as I was Jacob, I have also been Eve. And something tells me you have been as well.

Before we dig deeper into Eve's story, let's look first at Genesis 2:7–8, which tells us that right after the Lord handcrafted Adam into existence, He planted a garden and intentionally placed him there. He didn't pick a random spot on the earth. He crafted an oasis and placed Adam there to care for it and experience abundant life. The Lord loves to spoil us! After He placed Adam in the garden of Eden, He gave him only one restraint. Adam could freely live, move about, and enjoy everything that surrounded him except the fruit of the tree in the center of the garden—the tree of the knowledge of good and evil.

Immediately after this is when the Lord declared that it isn't good for man to be alone. He decided that Adam needed a helper. He needed someone who could speak life to his heart and steer him away from temptation. He needed someone who could experience the fullness and joy of life the same way he could. Knowing this, the Lord crafted Eve from one of Adam's ribs, and when Adam saw her, he knew that she was just right for him.

Leave it to the enemy to stir up trouble in the midst of something so full of promise. The creation of Eve must have royally ticked him off. I get it—now he not only has to watch Adam be lavished with God's fullness, but he also has to watch Eve as well. He was probably sitting there thinking, "Two little humans means twice the joy, twice the thankfulness, and twice the protection against my schemes." The grinch of the garden looked at the disgustingly happy couple and thought, "Challenge accepted."

In Genesis 3, the enemy approached the woman and asked, "Did God really say you must not eat the fruit from any of the trees in the garden?" Hold the phone! That one verse is so loaded, y'all. First, let's recognize the fact that the enemy spoke to EVE, not to Adam. Satan spoke to the one created to help her husband stand strong against all evil schemes. Bold, right? Also, notice the deceiver is already carefully crafting his words to manipulate Eve's perspective. Satan knows God didn't say humans couldn't eat from any tree, but he had to find a way to make her focus on the one thing that wasn't hers.

Eve replies to his crafty statement by saying, "Of course we many eat fruit from the trees in the garden. It's only the one in the middle [that's not for us]." Silly serpent! Part of me still wants to see her as an airhead in this moment. Why are you even talking to this fool, Eve? Run away, girl! She didn't, though. She took the bait hook, line, and sinker.

The enemy immediately responded with something along the lines of "Oh no, honey! God just knows that particular fruit is the most rewarding of all! You just think you're living a full life now. After you have this fruit, you will experience true, complete fullness."

Eve was convinced (Gen. 3:6). Prior to this interaction, she lived in thankfulness and contentment. She lived focused on the Lord and on being a wonderful helpmate to her husband. She thrived in the multitude of blessings the Lord lavished on her life. In that one moment of weakness though, Eve allowed Satan to shift her gaze to the one solitary thing God had not given her. At that moment, her contentment was compromised by her curiosity. She had never before noticed how wonderful the forbidden fruit looked. She became fixated on how deliciously satisfying and rewarding it could be to her soul. She was so focused on what wasn't hers that her thankful heart was silenced and her logic was deterred.

"She was convinced. She took some of the fruit and ate it" (Gen. 3:6). The Word doesn't say she necessarily believed the serpent's lies to be true nor was she forced to eat it. No, she was gradually convinced that this might not be a terrible idea. She allowed the enemy to tempt and manipulate her mind until he convinced her that the fruit from this one tree was what she needed in order to feel complete. That's a lot of effort, y'all! Remember all those middle-school years of trying to convince your parents you really were mature enough to go to (insert any sketchy event here)?

At this point in my reading, I remember thinking, where was Adam at that time? Soar in and rescue your bride, dude! But y'all, he was right there next to her! In fact, she gave him some of the fruit to eat too. You know in that moment that Satan, that slimy, slithering sleazeball, had to be thinking, "Great helpmate you made there, God! A real winner!"

The Word says that as soon as Adam caved and ate it, both of their eyes were opened. They suddenly felt vulnerable and started wrestling with shame. Was it shame for their literal nakedness? Shame for emotional nakedness, seeing their hearts had taken hold of something that was never intended to be theirs? Shame for spiritual nakedness, realizing their ungratefulness for all the Lord had blessed them with? For being convinced that God's perfect plan wasn't so perfect?

Later, they hid from the Lord because of this nakedness (Gen. 3:10). God replied, "Who told you you were naked? Have you eaten the fruit I commanded you not to eat?" (Gen. 3:11). I've always read this line in a tone of anger, but the closer I draw to our faithful Father and learn of His heart, I read it with a tone of mourning and sorrow, almost panicked, as in "What? Who...who told you that? Oh, beloved...tell me you didn't eat it. Oh, son...what heartache did you just bring into your life?"

Adam heard his father's despair and immediately pointed to the woman next to him. "'It was [the helper] you gave me who gave me the fruit.' The Lord asked the woman, 'What have you done?' 'The serpent deceived me [into thinking I needed it to be happy and content]'" (Gen. 3:12–13).

Imagine the heartache you would feel for your loved one if you had warned them of a looming danger they didn't seem to see, only to find out they chased after it anyway. You wouldn't be angry. You'd be devastated. You'd know what heartache and struggle await this wonderful human you love dearly. Worse, you'd know that there is no way to stop the consequences from playing out. They made their choice. But oh, how you'd wish with every fiber of your being that you could rewind time and protect them from it all. Now recognize that the depths of those emotions wouldn't hold a candle to the Lord's heartbreak over Adam and Eve's decision. He had to feel so burdened for his precious children, y'all. All this because they decided to fixate on the one blessing they thought they didn't have.

So I ask us, who told us we are naked?

Who told us that we are being robbed of a blessing?

Who told us that something happened that made the Lord remove His hand?

Who told us that our story is flawed, our purpose less than?

Who convinced us that He isn't good, that we aren't blessed?

Who told us we are naked?

Careful, friend, while we're so fixated on what *isn't*, the enemy is silently robbing us of what *is*. Though what we long for may be good and something so many others have benefitted from, the reality is that it may not be part of our story. While we throw a toddler tantrum and cry for fairness, our Father may be looking at us perplexed, saying "I'm not keeping anything from you, child. It was never part of your story to begin with."

That can be hard to digest—that the thing we long to see happen may not be part of the story we pictured. I'm still working to accept that simple truth. And maybe it will be one day. After all, God loves to shower us with blessings, especially when they align with His heart. There is no way of knowing for sure, which is the essence of faith. In the space between what was and what is to come, I challenge you to stay focused on what is. Don't let the enemy rob you of the joy, thankfulness, and life in this season. How often we forget that what we see before us today may not be part of our story tomorrow! But for today, it is. Let us not miss that beautiful, precious gift.

Rise up, sister. You have a choice to make—will you be a worrier in waiting or a warrior in waiting? The dream you dream doesn't have to die for you to be infatuated with the blessings of today.

Yes, Lord, we will enjoy this Eden and rejoice in what is today.

CONNECT

Pick one sentence/paragraph that stuck out to you. Record or summarize it below.

What was your first reaction when you read this? What emotions did it spark?

REFLECT

Can you think of an area of life (not your walk with Christ), that, at some point, you may have become trapped by to-dos and lost the passion you began with?

Pick one person that you are extremely important to in life and vice-versa—your spouse, your children, your parents, your friends, etc. How might you feel if they became dedicated to being there for you in all ways you need, but you could see that their love for walking through life with you had decreased significantly?

RESPOND

PRAISE. Name four God-honoring passions the Lord has blessed you with a heart for in this life.

1.

2.

3.

4.

REPENT. Name three areas of life (situations, people, passions, etc.) where you tend to become distracted by responsibilities and lose your focus of love, if you aren't careful.

1.

2.

3.

ASK. Name two areas that you need to regain your true focus of love with. I encourage you to dig for difficult moments and ask the Lord to give you fresh passion for these areas.

1.

2.

YES, LORD. Name one area you can anticipate temptation to become distracted and think of a realistic, tangible way to combat that attack when it arises.

1.

CLING TO SCRIPTURE

Above everything, love one another earnestly, because love covers over many sins. (1 Peter 4:8)

My children, our love should not be just words and talk; it must be true love, which shows itself in action. (1 John 3:18)

Be always humble, gentle, and patient. Show your love by being tolerant with one another. Do your best to preserve the unity which the Spirit gives by means of the peace that binds you together. (Ephesians 4:2–3)

Which verse did you find or choose that you will commit to memory and utilize as you remember what your most important focus is? Record it below.

Battle VII:
I Want You More

REPLACING THE DREAM
WITH THE DREAM-MAKER

It had been only seven months.

It had only been seven months of excitement, defeat, hope, anger, tears, research, mountains, valleys, and learning. Did I say seventy months? Because that's totally what it felt like. I was emotionally, mentally, and spiritually exhausted. I knew all of the cliché phrases of encouragement and reassurance held some degree of truth, but if I could have turned them all into actual stones to chuck back at people when they said them, I would have.

"Girl, you two haven't been trying that long at all!"

"God's timing is perfect. His plan for your life is unique and meaningful. Trust Him!"

"Chin up! After all, there are people who have tried and waited a lot longer than you have."

"There's no reason to be sad yet."

"Just lay it at the foot of the cross and forget about it. He will heal that pain if you just give it to Him."

"Girl, that is Satan trying to get in your head and take your eyes off Jesus!"

"It is your choice to let this hurt your heart this badly. You have to make up your mind and choose to be happy."

Hmm, all that sounds pretty enticing. Let me think about it. Nah, I'd rather ignore it all and stay a miserable cow, thanks. I changed my mind. I'd like to trade those measly stones in for a few bricks instead. What, too far? My bad.

Listen up, friends. I'm one of the select few females on the face of the earth that function more logically than emotionally. Rationally, I completely understand the pep talks, and I appreciate the intent behind them. I really do, but for crying out loud, don't tell someone who is processing a delayed dream that they need to simply "choose to be happy," like it's a switch. Like it's in their control. That's a bunch of boloney, y'all!

I know, I know. I do have a choice. However, I think it's a needed gentle reminder for all of you Captain Pick-Me-Ups in the world (including myself) that it's my choice to DWELL on those thoughts and feelings. I understand that it's a choice to stay stuck, but we have to remember that the pang of initial responses is not the same thing as choosing to dwell. We have to do better as women and stop making each other feel bad for being human. (Steps off my soapbox again.)

Month seven was May. It was nearing the end of the school year. My wacky emotions teamed up with the physical demands of closing out my classroom for summer, and girl, I had quite the hurricane in my heart! I was at the end of my rope. My steady hope had turned into disappointment, which then turned into panic and fear. Those feelings quickly grew into an annoyance with everyone and everything around me. They had turned into desperate longing. They had turned into aching jealousy. I was functioning on muscle memory, counting down the days until I could hide out in my house, away from the world and its demands, at least for the summer.

On cue, Mother's Day arrived, and it was *rough*. I really wasn't anticipating it to affect me at all. I was too busy with end-of-the-school-year stuff to remember it ahead of time, much less build up dread for it. But no worries, leave it to Lieutenant Butthead to shoot emotional cannonballs with such perfect aim and timing.

That morning, I had multiple well-meaning people ask me if I was a mother, to which I had to smile and respond, "No, not yet! Hopefully one day!" Now these were casual conversations in a church lobby on Mother's Day, so I wasn't floored or offended when it happened. I mean, geez, I live in the South. This usually happens on any given Sunday for women my age. I really don't think these comments and questions would have been a big deal had I not taken a negative pregnancy test that morning. That negative shouldn't have been a shocker at this point, either, but this one was different. This test was negative after a week or so of classic, early pregnancy symptoms. That single pink line in the sand was separating me from joining all my mom friends to celebrate that special day.

I guess it was partly my fault. I had combined my hope with my symptoms and had myself convinced that this was my double-line month. I was going to test positive on Mother's Day. How poetic! I had already daydreamed about how I was going to tell the world. It took everything in me to suppress my excitement and sleep that Saturday night.

Heartbroken, I sat in the sanctuary early Sunday morning—alone. People buzzed around in preparation for the services, but I was able to find a quiet retreat to calm my mind. I prayed over my heart that it would be in the right place to be joyful for all of my sweet mama-friends. That I would be able to stand at the door and greet with a smile and a hug, like everyone was used to seeing. That I would offer nothing but grace-filled responses to the innocent questions I knew were coming, as inconsiderate as they may feel. By the time I stood up, I felt confident that God had given me His peace and perspective. As I stepped out to welcome everyone, I was once again the beaming Jenna Oakes that everyone was familiar with.

As the morning progressed, it was fine. I was fine. Everyone had arrived, and service had started. I was a little numb, but I thought it was the Lord giving me the stillness I had begged for an hour earlier. We watched a sweet video about babies growing up before their mama's eyes, and it didn't catch my heart at all. Praise Jesus, this was going to turn out to be easier than I thought!

Y'all, I don't even remember what the sermon was about. All I remember is that by the middle of it, I had zoned out completely and was choking back tears. My mind was foggy and frantic, looking desperately for an opportunity to get out. My heart was racing, torn to shreds.

Physical crisis? I'm your girl. So far, fight mode is my natural response.

Emotional crisis? I'm gone. Peace! Flight mode all day, baby.

Logically, it doesn't make an ounce of sense—none, not one. Nothing externally had triggered this response. I know now that Satan was attacking, and all I can come up with is that I prayed so fervently over my heart but didn't think to pray over my mind. It was going nuts!

Comments made over the last seven months were flooding my mind. All of them—the positives and the negatives, the encouragement and the gentle stabs—looped on. It had turned into the white noise of my soul, drowning out everything happening around me. I tried and failed to regain focus and talk my heart down, but it was throwing quite an impressive hissy fit. In the midst of the storm raging in my mind, Brock's logic rang louder than it all. "What if that isn't our story?"

By this point, I wasn't even trying to choke back the tears that had formed and started to fall. I remember feeling like I had hit my emotional rock-bottom. I felt physically weak at that moment. I was completely spent. I hadn't realized just how much the longing was wearing on me, how much the striving was wearing on me, the carousel of hopes and defeats, the fake "choosing to be happy." I was just utterly and completely worn—plain and simple.

I distinctly remember sitting in my seat with quiet tears streaming down my face thinking, "I want to want You more. O Lord...make me want You more."

At this point in the service, the sermon was wrapped up and the closing song had started. It was my longstanding anthem—my Jesus jam! Maybe you've heard "Sinking Deep" by Hillsong Young and Free. If you haven't, here's the hook that I love to belt at the top of my lungs, despite the fact that I can't carry a tune in a bucket:

> Your love so deep
> is washing over me.
> Your face is all I seek.
> You are my everything.
> Jesus Christ,
> You are my one desire.
> Lord, hear my only cry—
> to know You all my life.[4]

Woah, buddy! Good stuff, right?

But I couldn't sing. The tears kept streaming. I had this overwhelming desire to run away to a quiet place and pour my heart out to Him. I was angry with our outcome that morning. I was tired of faking my contentment, despite knowing He had a plan. I was heartbroken.

I vaguely remember stumbling up to the altar and falling to my knees, weeping. Oh, did I weep! Every ounce of frustration, defeat, anger, fear, and annoyance from the past seven months poured freely from my eyes (and my nose). At one point, I felt Brock's hands on my back. He was battling in prayer for me, which made me cry even harder, which made him kneel down and wrap me in a hug as I sobbed. I felt absolutely no happiness in my spirit at that moment, but I was so overcome with Jesus and the peace that only He can give.

After the song had ended and I had stopped snotting all over the stage, I looked up to see that my Laura was on my other side, also in tears, waiting to engulf me in a hug. When I stood up, I saw a few of the other girls from our women's group making their way over to offer love in their own way. I get excited about being the one that gets to rally around my people when they need it, but there is something so refreshing and empowering about having them rally around you too.

---

4 Hillsong Young & Free, "Sinking Deep," track #12 on *We Are Young and Free* (Sydney: CCM Hillsong Music Australia, 2013).

I had cried all my makeup off, had swollen, bloodshot eyes, and couldn't catch my voice, but it was time to go greet for the next service. I was scheduled to be the lobby greeter, meaning it was my job to keep an eye out for anyone who may be new and need help. It's humorous to think about it now. I probably would have scared them to death! I really don't think I can adequately describe the way I looked, so I'll put it this way. Another member saw me in the bathroom before I went to greet, went wide-eyed, and panicked, thinking something dreadful had happened. Luckily, our pastor and friend ripped my name tag off and said, "Get out of here. Go." I wasn't ready to actually go yet, so I hid in the office for a while instead. Eventually one of the women who is a rock of mine sat on the floor next to me and spoke so much wisdom into my life.

Though I had been hit with a title wave of peace that morning, I was still wrestling with the whole guilt trip of "I shouldn't feel this way. People have waited longer. My logic and emotion don't match, and it leaves me beyond irritated." She just smiled and reminded me that no one else gets to tell me how my heart should feel. No one else gets to decide how much longing or frustration is appropriate during the journey. No one else gets to write my story. I don't even get to do that. (The irony of typing that sentence!)

As she continued to pour into me, I shared my heart's cry for God to make me want Him more. Honestly, I had been longing for my dream far more than the Dream-Maker. I wanted so desperately to be able to confidently say that whatever He had planned for me, for us, I was on board and fired up simply because I wanted Him *more*.

More than the dream.
More than the goals.
More than the plans.
More than Brock.
More than our children.
More than myself.

My mind and heart want that so stinkin' badly. Even today as I sit here and type my story, I long to be able to honestly proclaim that I want Him more than absolutely anything this life or this world have to offer. In that Mother's Day moment, I couldn't. In this moment, I'm closer, but I still can't.

Prepare to be humbled if you are ever bold enough to be completely raw and real with yourself. When you truly dig deep, past the Band-Aids on your soul and the knowledge of what you *should* believe, and ask yourself if your heart, mind, and words truly line up, you may discover some ugly truth— truth you didn't realize was your reality.

I've always thought I truly wanted Him more than anything in this life, but I've also never had a dream threatened. I've had dreams change, details change, people change. I've had dreams morph into different versions of themselves, but never before have I had to consider God may straight up tell me no. Never before have I had to label a burning desire I have as only a "maybe" and something completely out of my control. When the reins are completely taken from you, your true colors will shine bright! Mine, unfortunately, didn't match what I had claimed they were, no matter how I tried to disguise them as acts of obedience by "laying them down at the cross."

That month was a tough process. About a week prior to this happening was when Laura called me out for trying to control the uncontrollable with data tracking and research. There was a lot of revelation and dying to self that took place, and none of it was fun *at all*.

For a while, I had to practice faith through obedience and pray my heart would eventually catch up. Every time the desire to control our situation would rear its ugly head, I told the Lord, "I want You more." Every time I was tempted to feel longing, jealousy, or fear, "I want You more." Every time I held a new baby (and this was most definitely the season for new babies around me), feeling them melt and snuggle into my neck, "I want You more." Every time someone asked about my kids, "I want You more." Every time I watched our friends' eyes dance as they watched their children discover the world around them, "I want You more." Every time I felt little arms wrap around my neck because I'm an amazing, one-of-a-kind Aunt Jenna (and having to accept that it may be all ever I am), "I want You more."

Is it enough—to be a one-of-a-kind Aunt Jenna who freely pours out every ounce of love she has to give with no reserve or hesitation? Hard *no*, it's not enough. It will never be enough. But praise God, Jesus *is*. I have the one thing that will satisfy the gaping hole in my heart, the longing to rock babies of my own, and His name is Jesus. If you haven't found Him, TRULY found Him, and experienced His overwhelming good-ness—I probably sound like a crazy, cliché, Bible-thumping Jesus freak (and I'm ok with that). If you have, you get it. If you have forgotten, let me remind you, JESUS IS ENOUGH.

As I sit here and type, I don't know what our future will look like. When you are reading this line, will I have tiny humans of my own? Will I have little feet running around that I didn't have the privilege of giving birth to but am entrusted to raise? Will God reveal a different plan entirely for our family? I don't know, and that can be terrifying.

But it's also exhilarating, encouraging, and empowering. Because as much as I long for these dreams, God longs for me more. When I think about how eager He is to take hold of my fully surrendered and submissive soul, it makes my heart race. When I grasp that what He has planned for me and my family is far better and more fulfilling than anything I can imagine for us, it gives me peace. When I remember that I have a very limited perspective of reality and the big picture, it excites and calms me to put all my trust in Him who sees it all. When I remember who I was, where I came from, and how He has healed and redeemed me, it makes my spirit soar.

Whatever is coming, I want it.

I'm trading my dream for the Dream-Maker.

I want Him more.

Yes, Lord, I want You more.

ABRAHAM AND ISAAC

I'm sitting down to type this a month or so after I typed the previous chapters. When I sit down to write, I like to reread what has already been written in the section. It helps me focus on the topic and tune in to the Lord's prompting. Today as I read of my desperate longing to crave Jesus more than anything, it made me smile. God is so faithful, y'all. He has answered that pleading prayer tenfold. The doors He continues to open and the ways He is pulling me closer to His heart give me so much hope for the days to come, whatever they may hold.

I'd be lying if I said I didn't have moments where my longing takes precedence in my mind. I've learned it may continue to sneak up every now and then. I can see growth in those moments, however, because my responses of anger and defeat have been replaced with peace and excitement for what He's doing in our lives.

I wonder if Sarah ever felt this way. She was Abraham's wife. She was barren and had tried to solve her perceived problem with human understanding by giving her servant, Hagar, to her husband. (This may sound like our "Rachel" chapter to you. History does tend repeat itself, doesn't it? The two stories are VERY similar.) After years of jealousy and strife with Hagar, she conceived in her old age and Isaac was born.

Anyway, I wonder if, in the midst of the battle, Sarah ever made peace with the fact that she wasn't conceiving. I wonder if she ever decided to focus on God and trust that He knows best. I wonder if her husband made peace with the idea of it all.

I also think about what they must have felt when they finally looked into their son Isaac's eyes for the first time, knowing they were staring at a radical blessing from the Lord, a miracle baby, if you will. Was Sarah so overcome with joy and wonder that she sat dumbfounded, watching his tiny chest rise and fall as he slept? Did she weep? Did Abraham lose his breath as he looked into the face of his child, the promised vessel through which the Lord would fulfill His covenant? Did his knees buckle under the weight of the promise he held?

I'm sure they were completely in awe of Isaac. I'm sure Abraham was excited to watch him grow into the legacy he didn't yet know of. We know Sarah was protective of him. Genesis 21 tells us the story of when she had Hagar and her son, Ishmael, sent away after hearing them mock Isaac. Part of me wants to call her a crazy lady for that, but another part of me gets it.

Put yourself in her shoes. She was in her nineties before the blessing she'd always dreamed of was in her arms. I'm sure she was protective and eager and doting and joyful. If there was such a thing as a momma's boy back then, I can totally see Isaac being one. Can you imagine her panic when she realized Abraham was going to sacrifice their son, their miracle blessing, as a burnt offering to the Lord? No, I'm not making this up. If you're unfamiliar with the story of Abraham's faith being tested, let me catch you up. The story is found in Genesis 22, and it takes place sometime after Hagar and Ishmael are sent away. One day, God said to Abraham, "Take your son, your only son—yes, Isaac, whom you love so much—and go to the land of Moriah. Go and sacrifice him as a burnt offering on one of the mountains, which I will show you" (Gen. 22:2).

Before I comment on any of that—because trust me, I have comments—I want to remind you who Abraham is. Previously known as Abram, he was called by God to leave everything and go to a new land the Lord promised to him and his descendants. And he obeyed. Abraham is still known for his faith in and obedience to God's leading.

Back to the story of sacrificing his son. Let's look closer at this verse. There is no dialogue recorded, but the way God speaks makes me think Abraham did, indeed, respond—possibly with panic. This is another one of those moments when I try to imagine myself in this situation since details are sparse. This is how I picture the conversation going down:

"Take your son, your only son—"

"My only son? Isaac?"

"Yes, Isaac, whom you love so much—and go to the land of Moriah."

"Yes, Lord."

"Go and sacrifice him as a burnt offering on one of the mountains, which I will show you."

"Wh...what? Lord? Why?"

Silence.

Again, this is totally me trying to make sense of it all, BUT CAN YOU EVEN IMAGINE? The Lord acknowledges that Isaac is Abraham's only son, a son whom he dearly loves, before Abraham can even protest with those facts. Can you imagine how Abraham must have felt in that moment, realizing God was asking him to sacrifice the blessing he had waited literally a century for? That Sarah, his beloved, had waited so long to hold? What would she say? What would she think? What would she do?

I wonder if he slept that night.

I wonder if he cried.

I wonder if he wrestled with his flesh, weighing his options—deciding whether to obey or flee.

I wonder if he sat next to Isaac watching him sleep, feeling angry and betrayed by God.

> The next morning Abraham got up early. He saddled his donkey and took two of his servants with him, along with his son, Isaac. Then he chopped wood for a fire for a burnt offering and set out for the place God had

> told him about. On the third day of their
> journey, Abraham looked up and saw the
> place in the distance. (Gen. 22:3–4)

He didn't run away. He didn't hide. He proceeded with what God had asked him to do, despite what his flesh was probably feeling. I can picture him somberly going through the motions of preparing for the journey and the sacrifice.

I wonder if he felt that knotted stomach, barely-able-to-breathe feeling that overwhelms and accompanies heartbreak.

I wonder if he numbed himself to what was happening.

Could he eat?

Did he fast and pray?

When he looked up and saw their destination, did his knees give out on him?

Did he choke back tears and fake a smile to his son?

Did Isaac have any idea what was going on?

This next part is what gets me, though. Actually, it makes me smirk with holy confidence; it makes me feel bold and want to jump out of the boat. (That was just for you, Laura!)

When Abraham saw their destination ahead, he said to his servants, "Stay here with the donkey. The boy and I will travel a little farther. We will worship there, and then we will come right back" (Gen. 22:5). Did you catch that bold, trusting statement? He didn't plead for his servants to stay in prayer for them. He didn't drag the conversation on or stall their journey, dreading what was about to happen. He told them, "WE will worship there, and then WE will come right back."

I've read commentaries in the past where people understood these words as disrespectful, like Abraham was bossing God around—an early generation's name-it-and-claim-it style. NO, y'all! Those are words from a man who is confident that the Lord stays true to His promises. This was a man who acted in obedience because he trusted in the God who held him up during every other trial of his life.

Knowing that Abraham was confidently trusting the Lord through this seemingly impossible request, I have to wonder what his internal mantra was during this whole ordeal. I wonder if he remembered God saying, "Go and sacrifice him as a burnt offering on one of the mountains, which I will show you" (Gen. 22:2). *Which I will show you*—the exact words God used to call Abram to leave everything he knew and venture to an unknown land. The Lord didn't fail him then, so why would He start now? Maybe it was as simple as Abraham knowing that God is a God of Promise. If Isaac died now as a young boy, how would the Lord's promise of countless descendants through him come to fruition? It wouldn't. Perhaps Abraham had put these pieces together knowing God would provide an alternate solution, even if he couldn't see it before him in the moment.

As they prepared to venture to the altar, Isaac looked around and asked his father where the sheep for the offering was. Abraham reassured him, "God will provide a sheep for the burnt offering, my son" (Gen. 22:8). At this point, I know I would have been internally saying, "Okay, God. We're here. Any time now, reveal the real sacrifice. Whenever you're ready...any time now..."

When they arrived on the mount, Abraham built the altar and prepared for the offering. This next part is hard for me to imagine, and I don't even have littles of my own yet. "Then he tied his son, Isaac, and laid him on the altar on top of the wood" (Gen. 22:9). Don't breeze past this. When I picture Isaac realizing he was the sacrifice, I see him panic. I see this boy begging his daddy to stop. Did Isaac fight as Abraham tied him up? Was he crying those choking tears, where breathing stops and spit flies, like children often do?

Was Abraham weeping?

Was he apologizing?

Was he shaking?

Was he numb?

"And Abraham picked up the knife to kill his son as a sacrifice" (Gen. 22:10). Were his hands trembling and weak?

Did he feel nauseous?

Was he crying out for God to intervene?

Was Isaac trying desperately to find a way to escape?

Did he feel betrayed by his daddy? Did he cry out for his mama?

"At that moment, the angel of the Lord called to him from Heaven, 'Abraham! Abraham...Do not hurt him in any way, for now I know that you truly fear God. You have not withheld from me even your son, your only son'" (Gen. 22:11–12).

Did Abraham collapse in relief?

Did he sob and sing praises from an exhausted, thankful heart?

Did he drop the knife and engulf his son in a hug, even more grateful for him than he had been before?

"Then Abraham looked up and saw a ram caught by its horns in a thicket. So he took the ram and sacrificed it as a burnt offering in place of his son" (Gen. 22:13).

I wonder what life looked like after this event. Perhaps it caused problems between Abraham and Sarah, even Abraham and Isaac. Did seeing his father's obedience and faith, coupled with the Lord's provision, drive Isaac to be an even godlier man than he would have been before? Did he go through a period of wavering trust and fear as a result of that day's events?

One thing is for sure, I admire Abraham's faith. As much as I desire to want Jesus more than anything else in this world, I'm left wondering if I could have shown the same faith and obedience as he did. Trying to fathom holding my child, loving them, watching them grow, and then being asked to give them up for the Lord makes me sick to my stomach. Trying to imagine watching them cry out for help, knowing I was the one issuing the pain, makes tears flow freely. My sweet child...

I can't imagine how God must have felt as He sacrificed His Son, because that's exactly what He did. Jesus, His boy, was the sacrificial lamb for us. As the time of sacrifice grew nearer, Jesus pleaded, "My father, if it is possible, let this cup of suffering be taken away from me. Yet I want your will to be done, not mine" (Matt. 26:39). The love we feel comes from God, who IS love. We feel only a smidgen of the love He feels for us. Can you imagine how much love He feels for HIS SON?

Can you imagine the pain He felt as He watched Him cry out for help?

Can you imagine the tears God shed as He watched His beloved boy brutally tortured and murdered? The aching, tearing pain he felt as His perfect lamb took on the sin of the world and cried out "My God, My God, why have you forsaken me?" (Matt. 27:46) God couldn't even look at Jesus because of our filth that He bravely wore on the cross, but He still heard the voice of His Child crying out. I can't begin to comprehend it.

But He did it. God sacrificed His Son. Jesus sacrificed Himself. Why? Because He wanted **you** more than the comforts of this life.

When I think about how badly Jesus wanted me more than life itself, my soul is quieted. He took on all of my pain, fear, sin, and consequence—past, present, and future—and gave Himself in my place, all because He wanted us so much more than himself. He still longs for us. He wants us to run to Him and live in joyful freedom every. single. day. Why would we want anything more? Why would we want anyone more?

Yes, Lord, you loved us more.

CONNECT

What part of this section caused the greatest emotional response in you Summarize it below.

Why do you think this caused an emotional response in you? What did it bring to mind?

REFLECT

Have you ever witnessed someone you love lose themselves in longing or grief over lost dreams? How did it impact your heart as you witnessed their struggle?

Describe a time when desiring the Lord more than _____ seemed impossible to you.

RESPOND

PRAISE. Name four blessings in your life that God has lavished on you.

1.

2.

3.

4.

REPENT. Name three times within the past few years that you have struggled to put God before your own desires/dreams/plans.

1.

2.

3.

ASK. Name two areas in which you struggle to put God first. Ask Him to change your heart and perspective in regard to these.

1.

2.

YES, LORD. Name a situation in which you will commit to putting the Lord's will before your own, even when it is painful. What phrase will you remind yourself of when distracting thoughts and emotions arise? (For example, every time longing for our own child arose, I told Him, "I want You more.")

1.

CLING TO SCRIPTURE

I have been crucified with Christ. It is no longer I who live, but Christ who lives in me. And the life I now live in the flesh I live by faith in the Son of God, who loved me and gave himself for me. (Galatians 2:20)

He says, "Be still, and know that I am God; I will be exalted among the nations, I will be exalted in the earth." (Psalm 46:10)

My sheep hear my voice, and I know them, and they follow me. (John 10:27)

Which verse did you choose to commit to memory as you remind your heart to want Him more? Record it below.

Battle VIII:
Hopeful Abandon

IT IS WELL

Have you ever been around someone that was so at peace, so bubbly, so confident, and so happy that you wanted nothing more than to smack them? You weren't necessarily in a bad mood, but their energy was just TOO MUCH for you to handle at that moment? I have absolutely no doubt that a few people wanted to thump me in the head those few days after my Mother's Day surrender. I could see it in their envious little eyes. But I didn't care because if I was proclaiming that I wanted Him more than a baby, I definitely wanted Him more than any naysayer's opinion! Cloud nine was my new residence, and there was nothing anyone could do to change that.

The few days after God grabs your soul and pulls you in for a big ole bear hug are such special moments in your walk with Him. It's like the emotional high of a Disney trip, but way better. You feel empowered, determined, joyful, and at total peace. You are optimistic, energized, and you walk with an extra pep of confidence in your step.

After I left the pieces of my worn and weary heart at the altar, I was thankful to have my eyes focused on something other than the fertility app on my phone. I was so stinkin' motivated to start chasing after Jesus again no matter what because (picture me power posing and projecting my voice like I am on Broadway), I WANTED HIM MORE!

About a week after my surrender, I was hit with PLENTY of opportunities to choose Jesus. That's putting it vaguely. Let me rephrase, Satan had traded his sneaky water-balloon weapons for an arsenal of temptation snowballs and was eagerly waiting to chunk them at my blissful little head. These were not just ordinary snowballs, mind you. We're talking Alabama, not-really-snow-but-ice snowballs that bring tears and leave bruises. Y'all, if you aren't already aware, let me scream it so that you can take this nugget of truth and plant it deep, where you'll remember it always. You ready?

SATAN IS A BUTTHEAD!

Yes, I said butthead. I teach elementary school, so forgive me if this term gets your panties in a wad. You've seen the phrase and nickname sprinkled throughout this book, but I want you to really hone in on it as an undeniable fact, not just a touch of childish humor. When he is slinking in the shadows of your life, call his mischievous, manipulative, chaos-causing self out! I hope you can tell by now just how much his petty attacks irritate me.

Anyway, I anticipated these spiritual ambushes. The enemy isn't clever or crafty with his schemes, and I'm not stupid. Think about it, I had decided to lay down something I had been grappling with, something that had taken my focus off of what was truly important, and ferociously chase Jesus. I was taking hold of His truth and placing Him as the top priority in my life once again. Of COURSE, the enemy is going to try to stop, discourage, and ultimately send me back into the emotional whirlpool I had just been rescued from.

I knew this. I waited and anticipated his arrival, but DUDE, he came with vengeance! He popped my peaceful little bubble. It immediately seemed like every conversation, every stranger, every Facebook and Instagram post was a screaming reminder of my surrendered dream. And yes, I know, look for something sweet, find the nectar. Look for the red car, find the red car. I get it, but I am telling you, these were not coincidences. I don't believe in coincidence, anyway. No, these were strategic nets laid by the Butthead.

I was a ticking bomb this time, though. I was ready to fight back. Satan has always known which pressure points distract me, but he obviously doesn't know the Jenna Oakes that Jesus is transforming me into. He must not realize just how stubborn and passionate the Lord made me from the start. He seems to have forgotten the twists and turns of my story so far and how, in the Lord's strength, I have always risen above them. He must not be aware of the fact that I've grown into a better version of myself with each and every fall and fight to get back up, a version that is slowly starting to resemble my Savior more and more. He doesn't know that the Lord gave me grit and resolve to utilize when this world tries to tear me down.

He also obviously doesn't know of my protective, loving husband, who never has tolerated and never will tolerate these schemes. He doesn't know how long Brock prayed for me and waited patiently for God to bring "his perfect bride at the perfect time," a promise he's held tight to since he was a young adult. The enemy must not realize that this man of God I call my husband is battling for me behind the scenes through prayer. He prays over my mind, my heart, and my relationship with the Lord. He prays for my courage and peace and joy. He also prays for my future, our future, and for himself, that he will lead and love our family well. He is the epitome of strength and a force to be reckoned with when it comes to his family, especially his bride.

The enemy must have forgotten about my tribe. That feels good to say—my tribe. The tribe of women God has blessed me with in my adult years absolutely amazes me. I have my core discipleship band, consisting of three or four women who know the deepest, darkest parts of my soul, but y'all, I have an army of fierce, godly women who get royally ticked when Satan messes with me and who fight back by encouraging me and speaking God's truth into my mind and heart. They hear what's going on in my life and give Satan a kick in the teeth in the name of Jesus. It's an incredible feeling, to say the least. The enemy must have forgotten about them too. As much as the right hooks from my husband probably sting, I can only imagine how the enemy trembles when he realizes a bunch of angry and passionate, scrappy, high-heeled, lipsticked women are running after him, fully dressed in the armor of God. Anyone would be a fool not to turn tail and flee!

More so than anything, Satan must have forgotten who my Jesus is—the one who sees my broken mess and calls it beautiful. He's the one who searches for me when I run and hide, never stopping His pursuit until I am found and home with Him again. He's the one who wraps me in a bear hug and quiets my soul when I'm losing control. He's the one who was brutally murdered because the thought of spending eternity without me was too much for Him to bear.

When the post Mother's Day calm had passed and the attacks started weighing heavy, I started to feel a little panicked. My mind was trying to wander back to my old thought patterns of control. I felt my heart start to long once more for things that weren't mine to have, at least not at that point in time. However, I finally saw those tendencies to feel insecure, to self-deprecate, and to compare my story to others for what they truly were—tactics of the enemy, and I was infuriated.

I immediately rallied the troops, all of them. We started specifically praying for protection over my heart. We asked the Lord to give me heightened discernment to recognize Satan and his schemes. My discipleship band started praying for me, that I would accept our story, that my mind would be overwhelmed with joy and peace, that I would experience freedom from my expectations of God, and that my heart would truly want Him more than anything else in this life. Every time I was and am faced with a temptation to take my eyes off of Jesus, I remember my heart's cry of "I want You more."

After I issued a holy attack against the enemy, I reminded myself of the Lord's promises to me, and I clung to them like it was the last Chick-fil-A nugget on the planet. He has promised me that His plans, every single one of them, give me "a hope and a future" (Jer. 29:11). He has promised me that He is working in my heart and life RIGHT NOW, and He will continue to work until I am complete in Him (Phil. 1:6). He has promised me that no matter what this life throws at me, His purpose will always prevail (Prov. 19:21). He has promised me that anything Satan tries to use for my demise, He will redeem and use for good (Gen. 50:20). He has promised me that as I submit to Him, He will be faithful to show me the way I should go (Prov. 3:5–6). He has promised me that fixing my eyes on Him is true wisdom since things of this world are temporary and He is eternal (2 Cor. 4:17–18).

I wish I could say I've always had these nuggets of truth tucked inside my mind and heart, but the truth is, memorizing scripture is something I really have to work at. Throughout life, and especially during this journey, I have learned the power of boldly speaking the word of God into my situation. Frankly, I didn't know where to begin when it came to memorizing relatable verses. I didn't know Scripture that well! Good news, though, we live in the age of Google. Simply searching for "Bible verses about (insert topic here)" flooded me with more references than I could imagine.

If you can relate to any of this, I want to encourage you, Google away, girl! After you find those timeless words, take out that pen and paper (or make a note on your phone because we all know that goes everywhere with you), and save the verses that speak the most to your situation. THEN USE THEM! Pull those weapons out and speak scripture into your situation when old habits and mindsets try to sneak up and choke you. The Word will spring to life when you read it through the lens of a battle strategy, a lifeline of communication between you and the only One who has the power to offer you lasting freedom from yourself.

As the Lord walks me through different periods of growth in my life, I always try to target one main area. Sometimes desperation and busyness can be thieves of your pursuit. The theme of this current season of growth for me is, of course, "I want You more." The target I aim for is to find my yes in His "Not yet," to seek Him with hopeful abandon and answer whenever, wherever He calls.

Has my desire to have children disappeared? Absolutely not. Will it ever? Probably not. I'm still hopeful that somewhere in the cards to be dealt lies the blessing of toys strewn across the room and 2:00 a.m. wakeup calls. Have I abandoned that dream? Never. The Lord did place the dream in my heart to begin with, after all.

What I have abandoned is my idea of what my life should look like. I've abandoned the timelines I've set for myself. Sure, I still have goals. I still keep my ten-year dreams in the front of my mind. I still work toward them almost daily in some way or another. The difference is that their fruition in my life no longer determines my level of fulfillment; they are not my measures of worth. They are no longer the be-all-end-all details of my story. They no longer take precedence over Jesus in my heart.

It's sad how easily the enemy can blind us toward our blessings. We get so trapped by our limited perspective. Once these dreams took a backseat, I was overwhelmed with gratitude for what I saw. Not only was I reminded of what He has been faithful to lavish on me thus far, but I discovered new blessings as old dreams finally came to fruition. These were dreams that I had tucked away and labeled as what-ifs. He was calling them back to life, opening doors for me to pursue them. I was left speechless. I still am dumbfounded most days but completely ecstatic to see what He has planned next.

His promises are true.

His love is unwavering.

His purpose is fulfilling.

He is so good, y'all.

Yes, Lord. You are so very, very good.

ESTHER

The past five days have been an emotional rollercoaster. Brock and I are currently praying through a life-altering, God-driven decision. We feel like He may have called us to a radical surrender in service for Him, but we want to make sure this is actually the Lord lining up our stars. It makes everything a little difficult when you consider the fact that Brock is halfway around the world for another two weeks on a work trip. While he's gone, I am meeting with people and gathering more information. Our troops are praying over us, and we are trying to quiet our souls so that we can clearly hear His voice in the matter.

And oh, has He been speaking! The day after I felt the nudge to look into this, the Lord brought the story of Esther into the picture. This may not seem significant or even relevant to you, and I get that. What you should know is that God always, ALWAYS uses the story of Esther's to propel me forward when He moves. Every single major decision I have faced in my adult life has been tied to it. God intentionally uses Esther, in some way or another, to motivate me and give me clear direction in His leading.

I cried when the Lord brought her story into this decision the first time. My heart was racing! It was the first time I was confident that it could actually be Him calling. Today when He brought her up again, I just laughed. I am heading to the beach with my mom tomorrow, and I stopped by the store to pick up a book I've been wanting to read for some time now. It wasn't anywhere to be found. It should have been, but it wasn't. Do you know what was? A pretty canvas with my verse from Esther right next to the book *When God Says*

Go. I'm tellin' ya! I laughed, rolled my eyes, bought the book, and drove home with a wandering mind, tempted to call it all coincidence.

When I arrived back home, I ate some lunch and plopped my tushy in my recliner to write this section. I had planned to write about Mary and Martha. I even reread their story this morning. As I read the "It Is Well" chapter to focus my mind, I felt perplexed. How in the world did I originally tie Mary and Martha into this? No, something wasn't right. I jumped on the handy-dandy Google-bot to research different stories that could fit here. It wasn't necessary, though, because God bopped me on the head with the obvious—Esther. I threw my head back and laughed. OF COURSE, the last chapter of the book is about Esther. How fitting! I'm going to enjoy writing this!

I have connected with Esther in so many different ways over the past ten years. In this season of my life, I read her story, with better understanding that her life probably didn't look like what she had hoped for. But her story ended up being good, so very, very good.

At the beginning of the book of Esther, we find ourselves in King Xerxes's (it sounds like "zerx-sees") palace. This dude liked to party, y'all. Chapter 1 tells us about a royal party that lasted 180 days. ONE HUNDRED EIGHTY DAYS—that's an entire school year! When that was over, the king threw another party for everyone in the kingdom that lasted a week. The chapter also tells us that there were drinks—yes, adult beverages—flowing freely, without limit. This was for the men only, of course, seeing as it took place before the age of girl power. While all this was going on, Queen Vashti, his wife, threw a separate party for the royal women.

Remember all that alcohol flowing freely? On the last day, Xerxes sent for Vashti to come to the men, wearing her royal crown, so they could gaze at her beauty. She refused to come, and it made him mad as a hornet! (Esther 1:10–12) Now I think we should pause here. I've read multiple commentaries over the years. Some venture into the topic of submitting to your husband, but the overwhelming majority, especially by men, point out that the dudes were probably stupid-drunk. Gazing at her beauty probably meant her naked beauty, which makes total sense of her refusal to go, at least in my opinion!

Nevertheless, this made the king angry. It made the other men angry as well because they didn't want their women back-talking, following her example. (Go ahead and have yourself a long eye roll here. I did.) To make an example of her, the king exiled Vashti from the palace. The search for her replacement quickly ensued. King Xerxes issued a decree for young virgins to be brought to the palace, where twelve months of beauty treatments and pampering were arranged for all the potential queens. A year, y'all—a year of spa days.

Enter Esther.

Esther is the cousin of Mordecai, both of whom are of Jewish descent. When her parents passed away, Mordecai adopted her and raised her as his own daughter. Chapter 2 goes on to tell us that Esther was very beautiful and lovely. From the very beginning of her arrival at the palace, the king's eunuch favored Esther, giving her special attention. She was even given some of the best maids to see to her needs. As we read on, we learn that Mordecai instructed her not to tell anyone of her nationality and family background.

Let's pause again. Here we have a beautiful young Jewish girl. When she was a child, her parents died. My parents haven't passed away yet, but I can't imagine being young and losing them both. That was for sure a curveball. Luckily, her cousin was selfless and loving enough to adopt her and raise her as his own. They were exiled, which probably means they weren't living the high life by any means. Then one day, word gets out that the king is in search of a new queen. Mordecai hears about this and takes Esther up to be considered. Picture that, please. Imagine her sitting in the kitchen, doing whatever she normally does, and Mordecai rushes in, tells her about this, then hurries her to the palace with the direction to not say a word about their family or nationality.

Was she timid or brave?

Was she confident?

Was she scared?

Did she think Mordecai had fallen off the turnip truck?

After her year of preparation, she was taken to King Xerxes. Even though the women were given a choice of whatever jewelry and clothing they wanted to wear for the occasion, Esther dressed modestly and was still "admired by everyone who saw her" (Esther 2:15). The people weren't the only ones who were smitten with her! Verse 17 states, "And the king loved Esther more than any of the other young women. He was so delighted with her that he set the royal crown on her head and declared her queen instead of Vashti." What did he do next? He threw a party, of course! And declared a public holiday in her honor. I wish I knew how old she was at this moment. Even at my age, I can't imagine being able to process all of this. She's gone from exiled orphan raised by her cousin to the beloved queen. That was most assuredly unexpected! I'm sure she spent plenty of time thinking, "How in the world did I end up here?"

While Esther was adjusting to life on the throne, Mordecai was promoted to a palace official. He was good at what he did. He even stopped an assassination plot against the king! Sometime later, a man named Haman was promoted to a position above Mordecai. He expected all of those below him in rank to bow to him. Mordecai, being Jewish, refused to bow to anyone other than God. He had obviously learned from his Israelite ancestors' mistakes!

This infuriated Haman, though. He learned that Mordecai was Jewish and devised a plan to destroy all of the Jews in the empire. How, might you ask, was he going to manage to do this? Surely no one would be heartless enough to grant him the go-ahead in his extreme retaliation plan. Haman knew this, which was why his words were so cunning and manipulative. After crafting his little scheme, he took his "concerns" to the king.

"There is a certain race of people scattered through all the provinces of your empire who keep themselves separate from those of any other people, and they refuse to obey the laws of the king. So it is not in the king's interest to let them live" (Esther 3:8). Haman worded this to create the impression that he was defending the king, when it was truly vengeance for his wounded pride.

The king gave his signet ring to Haman, which was all the dude needed to make decrees. So the decree was made to annihilate the Jews, and they started mourning their fate. Meanwhile, Queen Esther was completely unaware of what was happening in the outside world. As far as she was concerned, everything was hunky-dory.

When Esther learned that Mordecai had been openly mourning at the palace gates, she sent her attendant to find out what was wrong. Was this not what he wanted—for her to become queen? Mordecai told the attendant about the decree and even sent a copy with him to give to Esther. Then "he asked Hathach [the attendant] to direct her to go to the king to beg for mercy and plead for her people" (Esther 4:8).

I try to think about what Esther may have felt when she read the decree. Was she angry? Panicked? Nauseated? Fearful? Did she feel guilty that she was living in luxury while her people were wailing and grieving? Yes, she could try to beg. She was in a place of royalty. She was highly favored by the king, but there was one problem. "[Everyone] knows that anyone who appears before the king in his inner court without being invited is doomed to die, unless the king holds out his gold scepter. And the king has not called [her] to come to him for thirty days" (Esther 4:11–12).

Can you imagine feeling troubled by something and not being able to go to your spouse without risking death? If he didn't welcome you when you chose to visit, you were done for. What if he was in a bad mood? What if he was busy? This is one of those moments when I'm SUPER grateful for living in this generation. I bet Esther was torn between heartache and security, fear and luxury. Mordecai was quick to snap the queen back to reality, though.

> Don't think for a moment that because you're in the palace you will escape when all other Jews are killed. If you keep quiet at a time like this, deliverance and relief for the Jews will arise from other places, but you and your relatives will die. Who knows if perhaps you were made queen for just such a time as this. (Esther 4:13–14)

Woah, baby! That last one is my favorite verse. The Lord repeatedly calls me to it, and I cling to it like the rare jewel that it is.

Talk about life looking differently than what you thought it would! Esther had gone from rags to riches. Was she about to go from a place of honor to her people's martyr? I wonder if she realized, as she digested Mordecai's words, that all this—all of her journey to be queen—was for this very moment. It wasn't happenstance. It was none other than the sovereign hand of God skillfully crafting the story of humanity.

Something sobered her up, that's for sure! Esther sent a request to her cousin, asking all the Jews to fast for three days and pray for her. "And then," she said, "though it is against the law, I will go in to see the king. If I must die, I must die" (Esther 4:16). Something tells me that when she was a little girl, she never thought she'd be in this position, with her family's survival riding on her shoulders.

I wonder what was going through Esther's mind when the day came to approach the king.

Did she hesitate?

Was she sick to her stomach?

Did she cry?

Was she confident?

As she walked to the inner court, did she have to resist her body going into flight mode? The course of her life would be determined in a matter of minutes. Would she find favor with the king?

Scripture states that she did. King Xerxes held out his gold scepter and asked what she wanted. I can't imagine the relief that flooded her body when he did this, knowing her life would continue on. When he did this, He said, "What is your request? I will give it to you, even if it is half the kingdom" (Esther 5:3). At that moment, I would have spewed every emotional word that had been bottled up for days. I'm sure she was eager to see him resolve this nightmare for her family.

As she began to speak, Esther must have heard the Lord quietly whisper, "Not yet, beloved." It was probably next to impossible to bite her tongue and wait, but she said, "Yes, Lord." She replied to King Xerxes, "If it pleases the king, let the king and Haman come today to a banquet I have prepared" (Esther 5:4). Her request was granted, and they each agreed to attend her banquet.

Did Esther have to quiet her soul to wait on God's timing?

Did she want to rush the process, knowing what was at stake?

At the banquet, the king once again asked what her true request was and promised to give it to her "even if it [was] half the kingdom." Once again, she must have heard the still, small voice say, "Not yet." I can imagine that at this point, her heart had begun to panic. Why was God keeping her from saying what needed to be said? She had been approved to speak. What was the hold up? Nevertheless, Esther said, "Yes, Lord." She requested that the king and Haman return the next day for yet another banquet.

Did she feel urgency and irritation as she continued to wait?

Was she confused or nervous?

Did she have a peace that surpasses all understanding as she followed the Lord's lead?

As if on cue, Satan slithered onto the scene through an interaction between Haman and Esther's uncle, Mordecai. Between the first banquet and the second, Haman ran into him and, again, became irate when the Jew showed no hint of fear or reverence. After Haman vented to his wife about the perceived disrespect, she suggested that he request to have Mordecai impaled so that he may fully enjoy the banquet without any physical or emotional distractions.

Little did Haman know what God was doing behind the scenes! That same night, the Lord allowed the king to have troubled sleep. Xerxes requested to have the history of his reign brought to him to read and, in doing so, discovered that Esther's uncle, Mordecai, had thwarted an assassination plot against him. He also realized Mordecai was never rewarded for it. Needing to right the wrong, Xerxes summoned Haman and asked his opinion about the best way to honor someone. Haman, being the prideful bullfrog that he was, named off extravagant ways that he would have liked to be recognized and honored. When he finished speaking, the king replied, "Excellent! Quick!...do just as you have said for Mordecai the Jew...Leave out nothing you have suggested" (Esther 6:10).

I love it. I love every bit of it. I'm eating up how beautifully this tiny piece of the gigantic story displays how God takes care of us, even when we don't know that He is doing it. At the second banquet, the king asked Esther once again what her request was. That's another one of the facts you can't breeze over. Xerxes realized her request wasn't for them to merely attend banquets. He also had to have known that whatever the true root of the issue was, it troubled her greatly. He didn't wait for her to bring it up, and each time, she was met with immediate reassurance that he would listen and grant her what she wished "even if it is half the kingdom!"

She must have heard God whisper, "Now, beloved. It's time." This was it. She replied, "I ask that my life and the lives of my people will be spared. For my people and I have been sold to those who would kill, slaughter, and annihilate us" (Esther

7:3–4). That was a super loaded response, if you didn't realize. She had not yet revealed that she was Jewish, but she did make sure that the king realized her life was on the line.

The way he responds makes me grin. "Who would do such a thing? Who would be so presumptuous as to touch you?" (Esther 7:5). Oh, Haman messed up! Xerxes loved Esther. We learned that early on. The thought of someone being bold enough to touch HIS queen made him burn with anger! When Esther told him it was Haman, he "jumped to his feet in a rage and went out into the palace garden" (Esther 5:7).

Meanwhile, Haman stayed back and begged the queen for mercy. Unfortunately for him, he fell onto the couch where Esther was sitting. Just then, the king returned from the garden. Oy! That was the last straw. All the king saw was what looked to be Haman trying to assault his wife. As a result of this abomination, the king had Haman impaled on the same pole the man had originally set up for Mordecai. It would be kind of poetic if it weren't so gruesome!

After the banquet, Esther came clean about her nationality and relation to Mordecai. Esther, once again, begged for mercy on behalf of her people. This time, King Xerxes gave her his signet ring and permission to enact a degree of defense for her people. What trust! He had given someone this ring and authority before, but this time, it was to a woman! I wonder what the men of the kingdom said to that?

What would have happened had she not listened to God's whispers of "Not yet"? What if she had tried to control the situation, eager to get on with the task and the story, and spit out her request on the first meeting? Or even on the first banquet? The king wouldn't have known of Mordecai's loyalty. Mordecai wouldn't have been honored. Haman wouldn't have been enraged to the point of building a prideful pole to impale the innocent. The king wouldn't have had time to realize how troubled Esther's spirit was. The whole story would have been different.

"Not yet" can be hard to hear. It can be hard to hear when plans are changed and when dreams are delayed. When our flesh cries out for answers, our soul can rest knowing that God, who functions outside of time, is already ahead of us, celebrating the blessings He has planned for our lives. When we remember that the Lord is aware of things happening now and to come, even those not on our radar, our soul is free to find peace in trusting His ultimate plan. We will be tempted to be flesh-driven. We may focus on and long for things of this life, but our spirits soar when we instead cry out, "I want You more!"

Will we choose Him? "If any of you wants to be my follower, you must give up your own way, take up your cross, and follow me" (Mark 8:34).

In the waiting, in the dreaming, in the mystery of it all, may you always choose to take up your cross and confidently cry out, "Yes, Lord," knowing that whatever He has coming for you, He is also eager for the glorious day He has planned to whisper, "It's time, beloved."

CONNECT

What stuck out to you most in this section? Record or summarize it below.

How could this influence your personal experience in waiting?

REFLECT

Have you ever fought against a "No" or "Not Yet" from God, later wishing you would have realized He was trying to provide, protect, or direct you? If you did realize it was God and listened, how might things have worked out differently, had you tried to control the situation?

How are others in your life indirectly affected by your response to God's leading, both when you listen and heed and when you ignore and try to control?

RESPOND

PRAISE. Name four times in your life that you can look back on and see why God allowed certain things to happen the way they did or how He ultimately used those times for your good.

1.

2.

3.

4.

REPENT. Name three times that you have been angry with God and His plan, even if you know it was ultimately good. Talk to Him about these situations and emotions, and ask Him to give you His eyes and heart about them, if He hasn't already. If He has, acknowledge and thank Him for the peace He's given you.

1.

2.

3.

ASK. Name two areas—past, present, or future—in which you have struggled to find peace in regard to the unknown.

1.

2.

YES, LORD. Name one area that you are choosing to work on truly laying down by saying "Yes, Lord" even when your flesh cries out in opposition.

1.

CLING TO SCRIPTURE

Give thanks in all circumstances; for this is God's will for you in Christ Jesus. (1 Thessalonians 5:18)

Then he said to them all: "Whoever wants to be my disciple must deny themselves and take up their cross daily and follow me." (Luke 9:23)

If any of you lacks wisdom, you should ask God, who gives generously to all without finding fault, and it will be given to you. (James 1:5)

Which verse did you choose to commit to memory as you remind your soul to cry
 "Yes, Lord"? Record it below.

SHOUTING YOUR YES

Every now and then, I choose books because the cover and title catch my eye and leave me intrigued. Sometimes, I choose books because word of it has reached my ears. Often, I receive books as gifts from others. Mostly, I choose books that delve into areas of weakness in my life, areas I need and want to improve in, areas I need insight and motivation to take control of.

Maybe you read this book in leisure and now feel warm and fuzzy in your spirit. God stories will do that, after all! Maybe you read this and have a new desire to refocus and run full force toward Jesus full force. Woohoo! You go, friend! Maybe you read this book and got nothing out of it whatsoever, but I'm going to assume that's not the case, considering you haven't put it down yet. Perhaps you're one of the beautiful souls who knows me in some way, and you were curious as to what in the world the Lord could prompt me to write about. Whatever the case, whatever prompted you to buy this book, I'm thankful you took the time to read it.

But I get it. What do you do now? You are one of the ones called to read this and are feeling the Holy Spirit nudging you to refocus on the Cross, but you're battling the reality that the dream, the waiting, the emotions are all still there. They're still hard. You're glad to know that someone out there had a Jesus moment and got their squirrels in a row, but it doesn't mean you can. You so badly want to do that too, but you honestly don't know if it's possible.

Oh, friend, I see you. I feel you. I am you. Actively dying to self can get frustrating, especially if your heart hasn't caught up to your mind yet. I wish I could tell you that as soon as you surrender, it will instantly get better, but I can't. As I type this, I've been experiencing many early pregnancy symptoms for a few days. Maybe so. I don't know yet, but probably not. We do this dance every month.

It's going to be a choice and a battle, but it's one you have already won if you trust in Jesus. You are already seated in victory with Christ in heavenly places (Eph. 2:6), and girl, if that doesn't light a fire in your belly, I don't know what will! Seriously, take a minute to comprehend that. Though our bodies are here—wading through the beautiful muck of life, fighting the butthead of lies, and longing for the day we get to look Jesus in the eyes—our spirit is already with Him at the right hand of God, seated in victory, simply because we said, "Yes, Lord" to His gift of salvation. There is NOTHING in this world that can change that fact or steal that victory from you. He wins, so you win. Y'all, IT IS FINISHED (John 19:30).

But girl, it is also hard. No one is trying to discount that. If I had to describe this past month of having to put feet to my proclamation of surrender, I would say it was the "most difficult easy" ever. However, this month has also been beautiful—so very, very beautiful. The Lord continues to teach me more about myself and my relationship with Him. He teaches me more about the woman He's called me to be and reminds me of the big picture when I become self-focused.

He has opened new doors and flooded my life with new opportunities, this book being only one of them. I have no doubt these are ways He is reassuring my heart that He's here. He sees me. He has me. There are still days when I sit down to write and am convinced I am crazy and no one could possibly get anything from this rambling heart of obedience. Then He reminds me that it's not my story that I'm writing—it's His.

As you hold this book in your hands, I hope you remember your dreams. I hope you remember how they make your heart race and your mind wander. I hope you uncover the ones you buried deep, thinking they were too wild to pursue. I hope you look back and celebrate the dreams that have been fulfilled, and I hope you never discount the magnitude of those dreams or blessings. I hope you find strength and courage to keep running if your dreams haven't come to fruition yet, if they've been altered, or if you're having to change what you thought you knew. I hope if you, like me, are exhausted from longing and striving, you will find your freedom in abandon.

More than anything, I hope you find the courage to lay those dreams at the foot of the cross. I hope you find the strength to loosen your grip and give them back to Him, the one who gave them to you in the first place. I hope you find peace, rest, and joy as you replace those dreams with the Dream-Maker. I hope you find the humility and boldness you need to say yes in the midst of His "Not yet."

And if by chance you have found your way to this book before finding the Dream-Maker, our Savior, Jesus Christ, I hope you seek Him relentlessly. I'm not referring to the Jesus our society may have contorted or used against you as a threat or a stab, but the one who is gently whispering to the innermost part of your soul right now. The one who is making your heart race and throat catch. The one who knows you more intimately than anyone else ever will and is waiting to lavish His overwhelming love on your life. The one who calls you beautiful. The one who is waiting, longing to throw His arms around you, welcome you home, and seat you in victory with Him. The only one who gives the rest you so desperately crave. The one who placed those dreams in your heart all those years ago.

Whoever you are, whatever your dream, know I am praying over you. I am praying over your journey. I am praying over your heart, and I'm praying that the day your dreams come true, whether you realized they were your dreams or not, you celebrate extravagantly, praise loudly, and share your yes with the world.

THE GIFT OF SALVATION

We're all waiting—for the answer, the dream, the cure, the change. Most importantly we are all waiting for Jesus to return and take us home. For this season, He may have whispered "Not yet, beloved" to the gift of a specific dream or goal, but He is eagerly waiting to flood your life with the gift of salvation, if He hasn't already.

What is it? Why do we need it? Who is Jesus?

The Lord created mankind, so that we may give Him praise (Is. 43:21). When Adam and Eve were created in His image, they were placed in the garden of Eden. In this place, God provided for all of their needs, gave them responsibility and purpose, and set boundaries to keep them protected and safe (Gen. 1–2). In Genesis 3, we learn that Satan deceived them, which compromised the protection against sin that God had provided. This choice opened their eyes to good and evil in the world and thus began the history of broken people in need of a savior. Our stories are riddled with jealousy and pride, manipulation and murder.

Later in Genesis, we read that after a few generations, the people were so evil that the Lord regretted making them. His plan was to destroy the earth and the human race. However, He favored Noah, the only man on earth who was considered to be righteous. He warned Noah of the coming chaos and led him to build the ark, which would protect him, his family, and enough animals on the earth to repopulate it after the flood (Gen. 7).

The flood came and went, and mankind started over. This solution was short lived, though. Generations later, we see evil has reemerged among mankind. This shattered the Lord's heart. He is the definition of love and righteousness and goodness. He cannot coexist with sin, which meant He couldn't be in relationship with the very people He created to honor Him. Desperately wanting to connect with us, He made a way for His people's sin to be covered through the blood of animals. Throughout the Old Testament, we read story after story of God's people trying to honor God's laws and falling captive to sin in the process, having to perform sacrifices to make things right again between them and the Lord.

God was still hungry for us, though. He was so incredibly hungry for relationship with His people, but as you can imagine, laws and regulations can surely put a damper on unhinged love. Why doesn't He just let it go, right? The catch comes when we remember that He is spotless and holy and cannot be in communion with those riddled by sin because it goes against who He is. There was no way for Him to fellowship with His people outside of the laws and sacrifices he set in place. There was no way to experience the deep relationship He craved with them while the relationship was dependent on upholding the law.

So He made a way. There would have to be a sacrifice that would be great enough to atone for all past, present, and future sin. There would have to be something powerful enough to overthrow the grip of sin in our lives, washing away the filth we carry as broken people. There would have to be a sacrifice so holy and pleasing to stand in the gap for us—one that would allow us to freely run to the Father, still broken, and be accepted and welcomed as we are so that He can foster a right relationship with us and redeem our souls.

He sent His Son, Jesus, to be this holy and acceptable sacrifice. He sent Him so every broken soul, every shattered heart would be free to cling to him for their redemption. Jesus left His throne and humbled Himself, becoming human for us. He spent years being tempted by all the sin we face, walking side by side with the broken people God so desperately longed to redeem. In His last years, He preached of the goodness of God and His love. He taught salvation through Himself for all who would believe. He taught of the relationship God desired to have with us and the way He would die to ensure just that.

This was such a foreign concept to the wrecked world that many considered Jesus to be blasphemous. Jesus was sentenced to be crucified—a criminal's death. He was tortured, brutally beaten, and ultimately murdered. As He hung on the cross, He bore every ounce of sin, existing and yet to come. As He took His last painful breath on this earth and released His spirit, our shackles of sin were unlocked and the barrier between a holy God and His broken people was removed. His sacrifice did so much more than just cover our sin—it erased it. Gone forever. God the Father now eagerly awaits our acceptance of this gift of salvation and the redemption that allows us to run freely into His arms.

Don't miss that, friend. He doesn't need you to fix anything about yourself before you run to Him. Nothing you have done, no weight of sin you bear changes Jesus's offer of salvation. There are no stipulations. You don't have to be prequalified or fit a certain mold. Your shackles are still on and closed, yes. The struggle, the anger, the fear, the doubt, the hurt, the shame, the guilt—they're still there. The chains are still around your ankles, wrists, and neck, but they're unlocked. Satan has deceived you into thinking you will be imprisoned forever. He's concealed the fact that you can actually escape, though life makes it appear as though you can't. Today, I'm telling you, beloved, you can be free.

God is a God of choice. He is not forceful, and He will always let you choose the course of your life. He's always been looking to the horizon, though, looking forward to the day that you will come home to Him. If today is that day, rejoice! All you have to do is accept His gift. Talk to Him. Don't be intimidated or think you need to choose the right words or present yourself a certain way—no stipulations, remember? He's been there this whole time. He knows you. He loves you—*every stinkin' part of you*. Don't feel like you have to put on a front for Him.

Cry out your hurt and your anger. Tell Him you're mad. Tell Him you have doubts. Tell Him you don't understand and don't think you can handle it. Tell Him you don't feel like you're strong enough, that you were cheated. Tell Him you don't deserve a new chance at life after what you did. Tell Him He made a mistake with you. He's God. He can take it.

But when you're done letting your soul pour out, look up. He's going to be sitting there, crying with you and celebrating the fact that you're finally running home. He knows you have so many doubts about your past, your present, and your future. He knows you don't feel worthy and have experienced the pain of broken trust. He also knows all the love He feels for you and how none of your dirt and doubt matter to Him because of Jesus.

Tell Him you have nothing to offer Him other than a broken heart and wrecked soul. He's so excited for you to give it to Him. He can't wait to hang it on the fridge, admire it, and feel excitement for all the things you will become. Then ask Jesus to come into your life, take over, and make you new. Tell Him how thankful you are that He died on the cross so that you can run into the arms of the Father. Tell Him you don't completely understand what that looks like, but you're ready to learn. You're ready for Him. You know that He died for you to make you new, and you are ready. You're ready to live in His love and make Him Lord of your life, even though it's scary.

Is your heart racing? Are you choked up? Is part of you so frantic to close the book because your mind is in overdrive? Are you holding back tears? Do you want so badly to believe the words, but you're terrified of what that may mean for your life?

What you're feeling is the holy battle for your soul that's taking place RIGHT NOW. God wants you SO badly, beloved. The excitement you feel in the pit of your soul that you can't quite place or explain is the Holy Spirit pulling you toward the Lord, calling your heart to its true home. The hesitation and doubt you feel is the enemy trying desperately to hold you back, because he knows once the Lord gets you, he will NEVER be able to separate you from Him again. Satan also knows how powerful a redeemed soul with a lot of dirt in their past can be for God's kingdom, and that threatens his evil agenda to keep the broken people of this world imprisoned in sin and shame. It's a battle—a battle FOR YOU. You matter that much to Jesus; He is warring for your soul, as we speak. It's ultimately your choice, though. Will you sit in your shackles, or will you let them finally fall so you can run into the arms of your Father and find rest?

I accepted His gift. Now what?

First of all, HALLELUJAH! I celebrate with you! Right now the angels in heaven are celebrating too! Luke 15:10 tells us that they rejoice every time someone is saved. They see you, little ole you, and they are loving every minute of this! Sometimes that is so hard to grasp because we can't see it. That is one of the beauties of faith, though—trusting what we can't see is truth, simply because God said so.

You are probably going to be on cloud nine for a while. Think of the one I was on after I surrendered on Mother's Day. That was surrendering a struggle. You just surrendered YOUR SOUL. Woah, holy fire in your veins! If you aren't feeling any different right now, acknowledge that it may be a bit of skepticism and fear on your part. That doesn't change the gift of salvation in your life, though. Remember, it's not related to anything you can or can't do, and there are no stipulations. I encourage you to walk in obedience and trust that you WILL feel it.

I have to be real with you though, friend. Many people who are new in their relationship with the Lord struggle when life isn't magically better, when things still seem broken and messed up after they've cried out to God. The reality is that we live in a broken world. Though WE are made new in Him, we still live in a world where the enemy runs free. Satan is still going to try to wage war on you. You will be hit with temptation. You will be hit with "life." Being saved by Jesus doesn't keep us from hard times in this world. The enemy will do everything in his power to try to get you to turn from God and think He isn't good, that He isn't keeping His promises to you.

THAT IS HOW SATAN WORKS.

HE IS A BUTTHEAD.

The battle for our souls will continue until our work here is through or when Jesus comes back to take us home, whichever comes first. However, the hope we have in Jesus is that no matter the battles we face in this life, He has already won the war. Ephesians 2:6 tells us that we are seated in heavenly places with Christ. This may not seem significant at first. But in Jesus's day, victorious warriors would sit to show that victory was won and the battle was over. It gives you a whole different perspective. Jesus is already seated in heaven, even though battles are still raging on earth. The minute we accept His love and gift of salvation, our souls are seated victoriously with Him. He has promised us that even though in life, we will have heartache, hard times, and events that don't seem fair, one day He will return for the final battle. He will abolish Satan for all eternity. All those found in Jesus will experience eternity with Him—pain-free physically and emotionally. We will live in continuous joy and celebration with our Savior. Paradise.

What if that doesn't sound good to you? Does it sound boring? Like you'll be missing out? Will you miss things of this life, even though you know you shouldn't? Still want to experience some things here? Yes, you absolutely will have moments where those thoughts creep up. That's Satan too. He's so crafty, y'all. Acknowledge it and ask God to transform your mind and heart to match His. Bottom line? Expect attacks. Expect longings for things in this life. Expect temptation. Expect doubts. Expect others to say and do things to hurt you because they're broken people too. Expect hard times, but don't be afraid to get excited for the joy to come.

Sanctification

The journey of sanctification is the process Christians go through as the Lord makes them more like Him. It's changing our lives, minds, and hearts to mirror His own. This will start today and continue until you are with Jesus in Heaven. Don't let Satan trap you with His lies that you have to be a "good Christian" to gain God's approval. He approves of you because of Jesus, remember?

Y'all, it took me YEARS to get this, because in this life, we gain approval for what we do. When you CHOOSE (it's a choice, an action) to seek God—to learn about Him through His word, to spend time with Him in prayer, and to trust Him to lead you in your everyday life—sanctification will happen naturally. He has given us the Holy Spirit to guide us. That's the still, small voice you hear in your mind and feel tugging on your heart when you know a change needs to be made. The Holy Spirit will convict you of changes that need to happen, and He will give you hope that something better is waiting. (If your conviction is paired with shame and guilt, that's condemnation. That's Satan. Don't fall for it.)

I also want to encourage you to find your people. If you have no one in your life that you can share your journey with AND WHO WILL ENCOURAGE YOU TO PURSUE JESUS OVER YOURSELF, hunt that relationship down until you find it! Your BFF who lived a life of self-serving sin with you is not who I'm talking about, even if they've found Jesus recently. You're not it for them, either. Find someone who is chasing after the same thing you are. Find people who are further along in their walk with Christ and can speak life into your new heart and life.

Find people who can explain the complexities of the Word, point out the enemy to you, pray over you, and encourage you to always choose Jesus. And listen very carefully to me, especially if you live in an area where cultural Christianity is rampant—not everyone who proclaims Jesus's name knows Jesus. Lean on the Holy Spirit to lead you to people you need in your life. The Bible is very clear that there are many people deceiving others about Jesus. CRAVE A GOD-FEARING FRIENDSHIP, AND SEEK IT UNTIL YOU FIND IT.

If you happen to have relationships that will prove to be more of a temptation than an encouragement on this new path, I urge you to step away from them for a season. It doesn't mean you will isolate yourself from people of this world forever. You just have to train, to learn how to use your holy weapons and suit up in the armor of God (Eph. 6:10–18) before you can confidently walk back into the battlefield. I don't know of any new Christian who hasn't had to make the tough choice to do this, including myself. If the idea of it all seems overwhelming to you, I encourage you to take a deep breath, look into numerous resources available to learn from, and trust that the Lord will direct your steps moment by moment. He will never expect you to do any of this alone, and He will provide exactly what you need, exactly when you need it.

Lastly, chase after Jesus more ferociously than your crazy aunt chases Black Friday sales. Set time apart each day to spend with Him and only Him. There is a difference between being saved and experiencing a deep-rooted relationship with Him. If you want to know Him intimately and discover all He has to offer, you have to nurture the relationship. Think of it like this: if you were married to someone, made sure everyone knew it, and were faithful but never talked to them or spent time baring your heart to them, if you didn't express the love and thankfulness you feel for them, your marriage would be nothing more than foreign friends sharing a house. We, the church, are Christ's bride. If we crave that intimacy He has to offer, it makes sense that He would want that too. Set that time apart and keep it sacred. Schedule it so He has your full attention. Not that you won't include Him as you go through your days—you will. Just set apart time for y'all to focus on each other. If you wouldn't be okay with your spouse acknowledging you in passing and half-heartedly talking to you for only a few minutes at a time, don't do it to God.

Your time with Him will be unique. Picture Him sitting next to you, and talk to Him like you would a friend. Jesus died so you can have this type of relationship with Him. Jesus and I have a coffee date every morning first thing. We spend about an hour together. Sometimes we read studies. Sometimes I write about what He's doing in my life. Sometimes I sing praise songs. We read His Word together. I talk with Him through my prayer journal. Sometimes I'm so broken that I just sit and weep, knowing He's right there weeping with me. There's no checklist for spending time with Him. It really is a relationship, y'all.

The only thing you HAVE to do is dig into His Word. Find a Bible (NIV, ESV, and CSB versions are great at helping new believers read and understand). Check the resources page in the back of the book for places to turn to if you need help getting your own Bible. Read it as the love letter to you that it is. It's the history of your royal family. It will come alive when you realize it's God's heart pouring into your own.

Beloved, I'm so excited for you to know you are stepping into His freedom. Your journey may not always be easy. It may not always seem fair. You won't always be on a Jesus high, and you will still fight many battles in this life. But, friend, congratulations—your war is finally over! Welcome home!

ACKNOWLEDGMENTS

To the small circle of family and friends who knew of this call to write *The Waiting War*, thank you for your enthusiasm. Thank you for your encouragement. Thank you for being the voice of truth in my life when the lies of the enemy threatened my peace. Thank you for believing in my ability to finish well and supporting me every step of the way. Thank you for locking arms and chasing the cross with me. Thank you for being my people.

To Kaylee Powell, my first rock-star editor and forever friend, thank you for coming alongside me, braving this new terrain and breathing greater life into this book. I am constantly amazed at your talent, your selflessness, your persistent joy, and your dedication to see others excel in life. Thank you for carving out precious time, week after week, to sit down with me and help smooth the rough edges of my written heart (and to Stephen for doing whatever it took to make it happen time after time). To see how the Lord used that time to develop not only this sweet story but also such a sweet bond between us makes me even more grateful for your yes to go all in with me. Thank you for bringing undaunted joy to this journey. Thank you for loving this dream as your own.

Finally, to my wonderful husband, thank you for your never-ending support. Thank you for twirling me around and celebrating when I hesitantly told you I thought I was being called to write a book about us. Thank you for speaking life into my heart when I battled self-doubt time and again. Thank you for your endless patience in this season, as I made this book a priority in our lives. Thank you for praying over every step of the process and bear-hugging me with shouts of praise and thanksgiving when I told you the book was being published. Thank you for seeing me as your crown. None of this would have been possible without you. Thank you for being an unbelievable provider in all areas of our life and truly loving me like Christ loved the church.

RESOURCES

Where to Find Help Against Domestic Violence:

- National Domestic Violence Hotline: 1-800-799-7233 or TTY 1-800-787-3224/ www.thehotline.org
- Database of Domestic Shelters: www.domesticshelters.org
- The National Coalition Against Domestic Violence: www.ncadv.org

Where to Find a Bible for Free:

- The Bible App by YouVersion—this not only gives you access to the Bible in all versions, but it also offers free study tools and an online community.
- Bibles for America: www.biblesforamerica.org (New Testament)
- WayFM: https://www.wayfm.com/bible/

BIBLIOGRAPHY

Evans, Tony, and Chrystal E. Hurst. *Kingdom Woman: Embracing Your Purpose, Power, and Possibilities*. Carol Stream: Tyndale House Publishers, 2015.

Hillsong Young and Free. "Sinking Deep," #12 on *We Are Young and Free*. Sydney: CCM Hillsong Music Australia, 2013.

Shirer, Priscilla. *Fervent: A Woman's Battle Plan for Serious, Specific, and Strategic Prayer*. Nashville: B & H Publishing Group, 2015.

Thompson, Elizabeth Laing. *When God Says Go Rising to Challenge and Change without Losing Your Confidence, Your Courage, or Your Cool*. Uhrichsville: Barbour Publishing, Inc, 2018.

ABOUT THE AUTHOR

Jenna Oakes has an aching desire to see and help others discover the Lord's heart for them. Through her raw, down-to-earth writing, she connects to her readers on a personal level—longing to encourage them to pursue the hope and joy found only in Jesus. When she's not writing, she can be found in her elementary classroom in North Alabama, where her family calls home.